Engaging with Muslims in Europe

Bert de Ruiter
(editor)

Publications

Bibliographic Information Published by the Deutsche Nationalbibliothek
The Deutsche Nationalbibliothek lists this publication in the Deutsche Nationalbibliografie; detailed bibliographic data are available in the Internet at http://dnb.d-nb.de.

ISBN 978-3-95776-025-8

© 2014

VTR Publications
Gogolstr. 33, 90475 Nürnberg, Germany, http://www.vtr-online.com

Printed by Lightning Source

Contents

Introduction (Bert de Ruiter) 5

CHAPTER 1:
The Spirit of God Preparing Our Engagement (Bernhard Reitsma) 11

CHAPTER 2:
Overcoming our Fear of Engagement (Bert de Ruiter) 22

CHAPTER 3:
The Socio-political Context of Our Engagement (Efan Elias) 34

CHAPTER 4:
Engaging with Muslim Women in Europe (Elsie Maxwell) 43

CHAPTER 5:
Engaging with Muslims in Mosques (Andreas Maurer) 50

CHAPTER 6:
Engaging with Muslim Youth (Anne-Käthi Degen) 58

CHAPTER 7:
Engaging with Asylum Seekers (Paul Sydnor) 69

CHAPTER 8:
Engaging through Dialogue (Ishak Ghatas) 80

CHAPTER 9:
Engaging Through Holistic Ministry (Hany Girgis) 88

CHAPTER 10:
Engaging with Other Believers – Establishing Networks (Bryan Knell) 98

Conclusion (Bert de Ruiter) 108

List of Contributors 110

Introduction
Bert de Ruiter

The arrival of millions of Muslims in Western, Northern and Southern Europe has permanently changed the continent. Since the 1950s Western Europe has seen the arrival of migrant workers and asylum-seekers, many from Muslim countries, that were formerly colonized or dominated by European countries. For the first decade the only arrivals were men of working age, whose main aim was to earn money to send back home and then to return home. This expectation never materialized, largely due to changes in immigration laws. They decided to stay in Europe and have their families join them. This radically altered the structure of the Muslim community in Western Europe which led to new social and religious priorities and demands on the host communities. In the Eastern part of Europe we see a re-awakening of the indigenous Muslim population. The Islamic religious institutions there are experiencing a renewal of activity, creating their own political parties, newspapers, cultural associations, charitable societies and intellectual forums. Islam is *in* Europe, and here to stay, albeit progressively and in different forms. Muslims have become the second largest religious community after Christians. Increasingly, is becoming part of Europe's social, cultural and political and religious landscape.

Phases of relations between Islam and Europe[1]

Looking at the historical relationship between Islam and Europe in history, we can identify several phases:

Phase 1: Islam and Europe

During the first ten centuries of Islam, the relationship between Islam and (Christian) Europe was marked by many conflicts, symbolized by the Crusades.

Phase 2: Islam in Europe, stage 1[2]

There are several waves of Islam in Europe that have left an imprint on Europe until the present day, such as: a) the Islamic civilization in Iberia from the 8th-11th century; b) the Muslim Tatars in the northern Slav regions; c) the dominance of the Ottoman Empire, in the Balkans and Central Europe for several centuries until the beginning of the 20th century.

---

[1] Taken from S. Allievi, *Conflicts over mosques in Europe. Policy issues and trend*. NEF Initiative on Reform and Democracy in Europe., Alliance Trust, 2009.
[2] This phase is omitted in the article of Allievi.

Phase 3: Europe in Islam

In the third phase, we see European dominance of Islamic lands. In the age of empires and the colonial period, Europe dominated Muslim countries. Later, during the ongoing stage of neo- or post-colonial influence 'at a distance' – through economic globalization, the pervasiveness of the mass media and western consumption patterns – Europe has gradually brought the Muslim world within transnational economic trends and political institutions.

Phase 4: Islam in Europe, stage 2

In this fourth phase, Islam began to spread in Europe through migration, beginning in France between the two world wars and in most European countries during the period of postwar reconstruction and economic boom – in the 1950s and 1960s in the centre and north and, later still, from the late 1970s onwards in southern Europe.

Phase 5: The Islam of Europe

In the fifth phase, we see the emergence and consolidation of an Islam of Europe through a gradual process of insertion, integration – initially in the workplace, then in a social and sometimes political context – and generational transition. This indigenisation process contributed to the formation of a middle class and an intelligentsia of Islamic origin that still has relations with the countries of origin but is born and socialized in Europe, building its own identity and creating its own space.

Phase 6: European Islam

The result of the process mentioned in phase 5 is the formation of a European Islam, with its own pronounced identity different from that of Arabic Islam or other countries of origin. This will increasingly become a native European movement, largely the result of a gradual and substantial process wherein Muslims are becoming full citizens on equal footing with other Europeans, with whom they share a common destiny. The outcome of this phase depends on the internal evolution of Muslim communities, the dynamics of global Islam and on the reactions and policies adopted towards them by the governments of individual European countries.

Today, most European countries find themselves somewhere between the fourth and fifth phases whereas in some countries we see the development of the sixth phase, which will become more visible in the future.

The integration of Muslims in Europe Muslim is an ongoing process. The internal articulation of European Islam is unfinished as there is a shortage of European Islamic theological leaders and many Muslims are still in the process of taking full possession of (their rights in) European public space, with many still considered fragile because of the difficulty and precariousness of their entry into the labour market.

We cannot speak of *Islam* in Europe, but only of *Islams* in Europe

I think that in order to understand what Islam is, one has to stop talking about a single Islam as a stereotype. Think of a palette on which painters put all the colours they are going to use – I would suggest that Islam, like Christianity ... has many different colours on its palette.[3]

It is important to understand that Islam is not a monolithic entity. It is impossible to speak of Islam in Europe (singular) as if all Muslims believe the same, behave the same, think the same, interpret the Qur'an the same, pray the same, relate to others the same.

Key characteristics of Muslims in Europe[4]

Generally we observe the following key characteristics of Muslims in Europe:

- *Geographically,* most Muslims are located in low-rent housing in the suburbs on the peripheries of major **urban** centers in Europe.
- *Demographically*, Muslim communities in Europe are **younger** and possess higher growth rates than is true of the European majority. The Muslim birth rate in Europe is currently more than three time that of non-Muslims. Research shows that, over time, the size of the Muslim families will mirror the overall European trend.
- *Economically*, Muslims face considerably **worse economic circumstances** than the majority of other residents.
- *Socially*, the Muslim community in Europe is quite **diverse** when we examine their ethnic and cultural background and their religious denominations and practices.

Some statistics[5]

The number of Muslims in Europe has grown from 29.6 million in 1990 to 44.1 million today and is projected to exceed 58 million by 2030. Muslims today account for about 6% of Europe's population, up from 4.1% in 1990, by 2030,

---

[3] Tariq Ali, "Why are we so obsessed by Islam?" in *Islam and Europe – Challenges and Opportunities* Marie-Claire Foblets (ed); Leuven University Press, 2008, p. 164.

[4] Robert J. Pauly, *Islam in Europe: Integration or Marginalization* (Aldershot, UK, Ashgate, 2004). Although Pauly focuses particularly on France, Germany, and the UK, his conclusions generally apply to most European countries.

[5] Pew Research Center, "The Future of the Global Muslim Population", *Projections for 2010-2030. January 2011.*

Muslims are expected to comprise 8%. Most will continue to live in Eastern Europe, particularly in Russia, where the number of Muslims is expected to grow from 16.4 million today to 18.6 million or 14.4% of Russia's total population in 2030.

In annual percentage terms, Europe's Muslim population is projected to grow at a declining rate, in part because of falling fertility rates and in part because Muslim immigration to Europe is leveling off. Nevertheless, the Muslim population will continue to grow at a faster pace than non-Muslims, which has been decreasing. As a result, Muslims are expected to make up a growing share of Europe's total population.

In 2030, Muslims are projected to make up more than 10% of the total population in ten European countries: Kosovo (93.5%), Albania (83.2%), Bosnia-Herzegovina (42.7%), Republic of Macedonia (40.3%), Montenegro (21.5%), Bulgaria (15.7%), Russia (14.4%), Georgia (11.5%), France (10.3%) and Belgium (10.2%).

Statistics can be misleading

We need to be careful in using demographical statistics, because they often do not give any indication of the religious commitment, beliefs and practices of a person. Some believe that only one-third of all Muslims in Europe actively practice their Islamic faith.

Persons of Muslim origin living in Europe do not all practice their faith with anything like the same level of intensity. Some people of Muslim origin have opted to follow the path of agnosticism or religious indifference. Others continue to be Muslim in a cultural sense, while paying little if any attention to associated religious beliefs. These are considered as a sort of lay Muslim population. There are no studies of any depth on the matter, but on the basis of a partial examination of the subject it appears that approximately two-thirds of the Muslim population falls into one of these two categories (non-practicing or agnostic, etc.) of Muslim self-identification. Only about a third has so to speak made their self-reference to the Islamic faith active.[6]

Christians engaging with Muslims

The presence of Muslims in Europe is something that not only concerns European politicians or the community at large. It should also be high on the agenda of churches and missions in Europe, who cannot ignore what happens to Europe and Islam. Muslims have come to live in our countries, cities, neighborhoods and streets. It is important to invest time and energy in engaging with Muslim on our doorstep. Unfortunately, at present only a small mi-

---

[6] Dassetto, F., Ferrari, S. and Marechal, B. (2007), *Islam in the European Union: What's at stake in the future?*, Strasbourg: European Parliament, 6.7.

nority of Churches and Christians across Europe have meaningful relationships with Muslims in their cities and neighborhood.

In this book, mostly written by members of the Ministry to Muslims Network of the European Leadership Forum, we want to help the Churches in Europe to engage with Muslims in a way that is honouring to God and that will encourage many Muslims to become disciples of Christ. In chapter 1, Berhard challenges us to think about the work of the Spirit of God among Muslims as a preparation for our engagement. In chapter 2, I address what I consider one of the biggest obstacles for our engagement with Muslims, namely fear. Because, our ministry among Muslims in Europe is affected by economic, cultural and political contexts, Efan explains the implications of this in chapter 3. In chapter 4, Elsie helps us to relate to the many Muslim women in Europe. Across Europe, we find many mosques; in chapter 5, Andreas gives suggestions as how to be a witness of Christ within mosques. Among Muslim youth, we see a culture developing that presents unique opportunities to engage with them, as Anne-Käthi explains in chapter 6. Besides Muslim immigrants, Europe continues to receive asylum seekers and, in chapter 7, Paul helps us to understand how we can show them Christian hospitality. Among Evangelicals dialogue, is sometimes seen negatively, but, as Ishak points out in chapter 8, dialogue provides good ways to engage with Muslims for the sake of the Gospel. Because Muslims are not just religious beings, but also normal human beings, Hany helps us in chapter 9 to consider developing holistic ministries among Muslims in our neighborhoods. Reaching out to Muslims is to be done in collaboration with other Christians. Showing the unity of Christ in action is an important part of our testimony among Muslims, as Bryan explains in chapter 10.

Christians and Churches in Europe are called to be agents of change and transformation in a society estranged from God. We cannot afford to be a bystander as Europe and Islam sort out their future together.

Our engagements with Muslims in Europe should be guided by God's self-giving love manifested at the cross of Golgotha. I suggest that churches and Christians across Europe respond to the presence of Muslims in our continent in a fourfold manner:

- With a compassionate heart,
- with an informed mind,
- with an involved hand,
- with a witnessing tongue.

I believe this book will help you to grow in such engagement.

CHAPTER 1

The Spirit of God Preparing Our Engagement

Bernhard Reitsma

1. Introduction

Several years ago, on the morning of *Ied il Adha*, the Islamic Festival of Sacrifice, the call of the minaret woke me at 4.30 am – early, but not unusual in Amman. However, this morning I could not return to sleep. Until late that morning, there was an unceasing sound of recitation and joy reminding everyone that God is greater: *'Allahoe Akbar'*. The atmosphere was almost like winning soccer's World Cup. I had always believed that Islam was a rigid, joyless and even boring religion, yet here I was, confronted with an explosion of religious joy.

Through this experience a lingering question forced itself upon me with new vigour. What is the meaning of religious experiences of people who do not know Christ, yet seem to be in touch with the Divine? In conservative protestant and evangelical circles, this issue is rarely addressed. In relation to Islam especially, all emphasis is on dogmatic questions such as the uniqueness of Christ, the Sonship of Jesus, the Trinity and the meaning of revelation. Yet the spirituality of Muslims is as much an issue as doctrine. How do we interpret that in the light of the Gospel? We confess that there is no other name under heaven given among men by which we must be saved (Acts 4:12 ESV).

In general, we believe that Christian spirituality has to do with experiencing the only true God, the Father of Jesus Christ. Does that then suggest that the religious experiences of others are simply false or misleading? What about Buddhists that meditate, Jews that ecstatically celebrate Simchat Torah (the feast of the Torah) or, for that matter, Muslims that exuberantly commemorate Abraham's willingness to sacrifice his son. Christians usually connect their spirituality and religious experience with the Spirit of God, but what about the religious experiences of non-Christians? What if Muslims' prayers are being answered? Are they completely disconnected from the Holy Spirit? And if not, then what does that connection look like?

These questions kept me occupied on that early morning and deserve further thought. In trying to interpret the religious experiences of Muslims,[1] my start-

---

[1] Here I limit myself to the religious experiences of Muslims, although the same question could be asked concerning adherents of other religions. However, Islam and Christianity share their faith in one single and 'personal' God.

ing point is Romans 8, one of the most poignant New Testament expositions of the person and work of the Holy Spirit.[2]

2. The Spirit as the Spirit of Christ (Rom. 8)

In Romans 8, Paul discusses the person and work of the Spirit in the context of the opposition of the two ages, the old and the new aeon.[3] With respect to the ages, it is not the element of time that is conclusive, but the aspect of power and dominion. The old age, that entered the world with Adam (Rom. 5:12-14, 17), is the era that is determined by the powers of sin, death and the flesh. These powers collaborate to form a deadly coalition and in this they are able to misuse the Torah (Rom. 7:13-26). Although the Torah in itself is good and holy (Rom. 7:12), it is compelled to contribute to the evil scheme of the powers of the old age. In a world dominated by sin, the Law can only point out sin and condemn the sinner to death (Rom. 6).[4]

Over against this regime of sin, death and the flesh, we find the new life through the Spirit (Rom. 8:2). The coming of Christ is the watershed in history, the turning point of the ages. (cf. Rom. 6; 7:1-6; 8:1). God has ultimately and decisively acted in history by sending His son and by definitively eliminating sin in Him on the cross (Rom. 8:2, 3). The old age has yielded to the new, the eschaton is here, the last days have arrived. Righteousness now replaces sin (Rom. 6:13, 18-20), life replaces death, grace replaces the law (Rom. 6:14) and the Spirit replaces the flesh (Rom. 8:3-9). Instead of sin the Spirit now lives in believers (cf. Rom. 7:20 and 8:9, 11). He ensures that the new life he brings is actually lived. Under the old regime of sin and death, the law could not be fulfilled; now the righteous requirement of the law is being fulfilled in the heart of believers (Rom. 8:4). In baptism, they have died with Christ to the powers of the old regime in order that – raised with Him – they would walk in newness of life (Rom. 6:4); they are death to sin and alive to God in Jesus

---

[2] We should be careful not to call it a systematic exposé, since even Paul's letter to the Romans was a 'word on target', written in a specific situation for a specific occasion (Cf. B.J.G. Reitsma, *Geest en schepping. Een bijbels-theologische bijdrage aan de systematische doordenking van de verhouding van de Geest van God en de geschapen werkelijkheid*, Zoetermeer 1997). Nevertheless, the letter is basic for Paul in that sense, that he carefully explains here the core elements of the Gospel he preached, cf. Reitsma, *Geest en schepping*. p. 68 n. 3. Within the letter, Chapter 8 is again essential as far as it concerns the Spirit of God, p. 68 n. 2.

[3] Paul does not use the terminology of the two aeons here, but does refer to that part of the worldview of the second temple period that speaks about the olam haze and the olam haba, cf. Reitsma, pp. 70-71. Cf. pp. 69-120, specifically pp. 69-80, concerning the two ages in Romans 5-8.

[4] Cf. Reitsma, pp. 71-73.

Christ (Rom. 6:11). Through and in the death of Christ they have been released from the law that held them captives, to be raised in freedom to serve in the new way of the Spirit (Rom. 6:17, 18; 7:6). In short, sin has lost its power over them; it is the Spirit that now rules over their lives.

Paul emphasizes with great force that these two regimes are absolute and mutually exclude each other. Someone is a slave – either of sin which leads to death, or of obedience, which leads to righteousness (Rom. 6:16); someone lives either according to the flesh or according to the Spirit (Rom. 8:5-9). For 'the mind that is set on the flesh is hostile to God' (Rom. 8:7) but 'those who belong to Christ Jesus have crucified the flesh with its passions and desires' (Gal. 5:24) and have become slaves of righteousness (Rom. 6:18). Anyone who is in Christ, is a new creation (2 Cor. 5:17).

With this, Paul does not want to claim that sin does not exist for the believer. The powers of the old age have not completely disappeared and their influence is present until today. The body is dead because of sin (Rom. 8:10) and mortal (Rom. 8:11). Although the believer is a child of God and therefore an heir, the inheritance is still awaiting (Rom. 8:17, 23). Reality is marked by the tension between old and new. However, this does not mean that the two sides are in balance. The presence of the new life does not compare to the remnants of the old. The present is the transition from one age to the other. Through the cross and the resurrection of Christ the sufferings of this present time serve the coming of the new life. The whole creation is groaning together in the pains of *childbirth*. In other words, the pain of the present time leads to new life, not to death. It is the sign that something new is about to break through, the fullness of the glory of God (cf. Rom. 8:18, 23).

The Spirit works in this tension in two ways. First, He bestows upon the world new life in Christ. In the Spirit, the eschatological glory is already present. The Spirit is the new authority that rules over the believers and the Christian community. Secondly and simultaneously, the Spirit unmasks the old age as a reality that has been alienated from God, as a regime of sin and death. By revealing life in the midst of the old aeon, He also convicts the creation that has been subjected to futility (Rom. 8:20). Everything is being judged according to the measure of the cross of Christ.[5]

By characterizing the Spirit as the predominant power and inaugurator of the new regime, Paul has decisively defined the Spirit as the Spirit of Christ (Rom. 8:9). We can only refer to the Spirit and His work in relation to Christ. Only through Him and the aeon that has begun in Him we can discern and identify the Spirit of God.

---

[5] Reitsma, pages 117-118, 159, 160.

The above implies that it is impossible to disconnect the 'universal' work of the Spirit from Christ. The Spirit that according to Genesis 1:2 hovered over the face of the waters, that filled the craftsmen of the tabernacle (Ex. 35:31) and that makes the whole creation live (Ps. 104:30), is none other than the Spirit we have come to know through Christ. It goes without saying that in the time of the Old Testament this was not disclosed in the same way as in the New Testament. We cannot erase salvation history. Still, the person and work of Christ is central to a Christian understanding of reality. He is the one that qualifies our life, our thinking and our theologizing. He is the frame of reference. Therefore, everything we presume to know and try to express, always has to be related to Christ. It is similar to the relationship I have with my wife. I cannot speak about her other than as the one that I married. I cannot pretend to see her in any other way. Even when I look at a picture of her as a child, it remains a picture of my wife. Strictly speaking, that would be an anachronism, but there is no other way I can refer to her than as my wife. In a similar way, we can only refer to the Spirit and His work in the whole cosmos from the perspective of our relationship with Christ.[6] We cannot refer to the Spirit apart from how we have come to know Him in Christ.

An important question is whether this Christological starting point is too unbalanced. Does such a Christocentric approach in mission not overrule any other perspective? Is it, in my model still possible to relate the particular and critical story of Christ to the wider reality of this world?[7] Can we somehow bring together the critical moment of the Cross of Christ and the plurality of people with different cultures and religions? Or is that, in a Christocentric approach simply impossible? Would a more Trinitarian model not be more helpful?[8]

In my view, the problem is not so much a Christocentric (or better: Christ-centered) approach, but a Christomonistic approach. Christomonism basically states that Christ is the single and only representation of God. There is no more God than Christ. That does not leave room for a Trinitarian view of God

---

[6] Christ was also bearer of the Spirit. H. Berkhof pointed this out in his Christian Theology, Grand Rapids Michigan: Eerdmans 2004, second edition and his *De leer van de Heilige Geest*, Nijkerk 1964. However, even that work of the Spirit can only be approached from the end. The Spirit that led Christ into the wilderness and filled Him with His presence is the Spirit that through Christ was sent into the world and started to work in a new and complete way in the world.

[7] That has always been the criticism of the Orthodox tradition of the filioque in the Nicene creed. That would leave too little room for the universal and independent work of the Spirit in creation and practically identifies the Spirit with Christ. The Spirit then becomes just another word for Christ.

[8] Cf. Van 't Kruis, p. 14, 15, 85, 87.

and should indeed be renounced as heretic. A Christocentric or Christ-centered approach, however, does not contradict a Trinitarian understanding of God; it emphasizes that God can only be known through Christ, and that He revealed himself ultimately and fully in Him. When we emphasize Christ as the centre, it is an epistemological approach, not an ontological approach. Christ and God do not completely coincide.

A Christomonistic approach indeed does not leave any room for the contextuality of theology, nor for the importance of different cultures and situations. Christocentrism, however, does, at least as long as *Christ* is truly the center of our thinking and not our Western, Eastern or Southern *ideas* and *interpretations* of Christ.[9] Who *Christ* really is, can only be revealed together with all cultures and contexts. Moreover, the identity of God in Christ will even receive clearer distinctness in the encounter with other religions. In this way, we will also become aware of the contextuality of our own theology.

The fundamental question, therefore, remains how the Spirit of Christ is present in the world, in cultures and religions. There is a tension between the confession that the Spirit is the Spirit of Christ and the claim that the Spirit works in the whole cosmos, since this whole cosmos is still the place where the powers of the old aeon are present. In the light of Romans 8, I would say that the Spirit at work in the whole creation, is the Spirit of Christ and cannot therefore simply be identified with everything that takes places in a creation where the powers of the old age are still at large.[10] It is especially here that there is a danger of spiritual colonialism, of annexing the Spirit with our own ideologies and views, of identifying the work of the Spirit with our work. Throughout history, almost everything has been claimed as spiritually justified, from slavery to the abolition of slavery, from apartheid to the ending of apartheid, from communism to the fall of the Berlin wall, from capitalism to socialism. In this way, the Spirit is in danger of becoming an anti-spirit.[11]

It is only in the light of the cross that we can see how God is present in this world. What the world perceives as the end, for God is the beginning. Living for God starts with dying to the world. Only through death is God's Kingdom realized. And

---

[9] The danger that christocentric universalism is identified with Western thinking is still real. But this is not only a Western problem. All cultures struggle with the tension between their culturally influenced interpretation of the Gospel and the essence of the Gospel. It is true, however, that especially the West needs to be alert, because of its history and the still seemingly dominant position of western theology in the world.

[10] Cf. Reitsma, p. 118, pp. 168-171.

[11] Cf. the profound reasoning of K. Barth in KD III/1 pp. 115-120, esp. pp. 118-119; cf. Reitsma, pp. 51-53.

only he who acknowledges that God works where no one expects it and no one will recognize it will discover something of the work of the Spirit in the whole cosmos.

3. Non-Christian spirituality and the Spirit of Christ

In this context, we understand religious experience as something that touches the deeper levels of one's existence. It is not something in which people are unconsciously subject to an outside force, in which their personality is temporarily taken over. That might be possible, but is not the norm. Even someone who could be called possessed, frantic or under influence, is not without some form of control. Whenever we consider the relationship between the Spirit and religious experiences, it is important to realize this. Experience is not simply thé sign that the Spirit is working as if the Spirit is not working when people lack these experiences. The Spirit never completely takes over our individuality. That is first of all given with the distinction between God and creation. The Creator and the creation can never be completely identified and remain distinct. Secondly, in line with Jesus' statement that His Kingdom cannot be forced upon people (John 18:36), the Spirit will always respect the freedom and individuality of each person. Spiritual experiences therefore always are a *human* response to the work of God; it is an interaction between humanity and the divine.

Christianity is a monotheistic religion and central to it is the confession that there is only one God (Deut. 6:4; 1 Kor. 8:4-6), Creator of heaven and earth, the God of Abraham, Isaak and Jacob, the Father of Jesus Christ. Christianity has also always confessed to the omnipresence of God: this Creator is present everywhere through his Spirit. If both premises are true, than we cannot escape the conclusion that all religious experiences somehow have to be connected/related to God in some way as well. The question is: how?

My thesis is that religious experiences are all human responses to the presence and the work of God through his Spirit in this world. There are only two other options. Either religious experiences are purely internal human and psychological phenomena, or they are occurrences that are inspired by the evil one, although even then we could not consider this as completely outside of a person's individuality. Both suggestions might have a kernel of truth, but do not exclude my claim that all religious experiences somehow are reaction to God's presence.

Even when religious experience is a purely psychological phenomenon and people are completely isolated from external influence, they are still responding to God's presence, albeit by secluding themselves from His loving presence. It is still the experience of people who are created by God and for God and who can only live on the breath of His Spirit. That is confirmed by the fact that certain psychological phenomena have a religious flavor. Anthropology and psychology imply theology.

In a different way, the same applies for viewing religious experience as the work of the evil one. Apart from the fact that it is impossible to reduce all non-Christian religions and their religious experience to Satan, even then Satanism is also a reaction to the Creator, but in an antithetical and adverse way. It is the complete rejection of the one and only true God. It is the experience in which people completely seclude themselves from Him and open themselves up for the evil one. And even this creature only lives by the grace of God's mercy and longsuffering.

When we assert that religious experiences are reactions to God's presence in this world, it does not imply, that all these experiences are 'good' or 'true' or contain 'truth', or even that they are inspired by the Spirit of God. My point is that they somehow have to do with the Spirit of God. However, as long as Christ is excluded from these experiences, we have to emphasize that they are imperfect or incomplete or even deformed and corrupted. After all, the Spirit is the Spirit of Christ and where Christ is absent, the source of all spirituality is fading. Through the flesh, the self, or the misleading of Satan or the influence of sin the source of the Spirit can even become unrecognizable. A rebellious heart, persistent presuppositions or past occurrences or traumas could hinder a person to really acknowledge and experience the depth of Gods nature and character in Christ. He is after all the final and ultimate revelation of God's being and only in Him all religious experiences find their true meaning. It is in this respect interesting to notice that God continues to bestow all human beings with his goodness. 'For he makes his sun rise on the evil and on the good, and sends rain on the just and on the unjust' (Mat. 5:45). In analogy, the same can be said about spiritual experiences. The question is how human beings respond to this goodness of God. Paul emphasizes that the root problem in the world is, that human beings do not acknowledge God's goodness: they do not honor him as God or give thanks to him (Rom. 1:21).

As we have seen in Romans 8 the Spirit works in two ways. One the one hand, He establishes the new life in Christ; on the other, He convicts the old life outside of Christ as sinful and corrupted. New life only dawns at the other side of the grave, through death, in baptism. Therefore, we could also conclude that the Spirit works in a doual manner in relation to religious experiences. On the one hand, whenever the Spirit evokes religious responses in people, He always points people to Christ. The Spirit wants people to experience the blessings of Christ. And whoever opens up to the presence of the Spirit will find that Christ will become more central in life. Christ is and remains the benchmark for all experiences. By Him they are being tested, purified, cleansed and renewed.

On the other hand, the work of the Spirit also convicts experiences that are void of Christ. The coming of the Spirit is never only affirming, it also creates a crisis. Every experience that conflicts with the fullness of the Gospel in Jesus

Christ is critiqued by the cross. Whatever is believed or experienced is not neutral. Every corrupted and imperfect experience needs to be renewed. Wherever the Spirit is at work and receives space, there will always be a breaking point as well. A transition from a non-Christian religion to faith in Christ always involves a turning point, which is never smooth and fluid.

This break with the past does not, however, imply that the past is erased. Transition to faith in Christ is through dying and rising with Christ, yet an individual with all his experiences remains recognizable and does not lose his or her identity. Simon Peter might have been a completely new person after Pentecost, we can still distinguish Peter's character and identity. The same is true for Paul, who, after his conversion on the road to Damascus, still displays a similar zeal as before, but now as a regenerated person for Christ. Radically new as it is, in the recreation God does not start all over again, as if there has not been anything before.[12] Through baptism there is both continuity and discontinuity in the life of the believer. The same is true, in my view, for spiritual experiences from the past: they will not completely be set aside, but renewed. As the grain of wheat needs to die in order to bear fruit, likewise the religious experiences of individuals need to die with Christ in order to bear fruit for Him. It is *their* specific experiences that die with them in Christ, but it is also true that *these same* experiences will be raised again with Christ.

That can even be true of certain outright negative experiences, in which people have secluded themselves completely from God. These experiences can become meaningful exactly in their adverse character. The light of the Spirit can project a new image from this negative picture and, in this way, even these experiences can, through dying with Christ, become reflections of God's glory. As Paul's religious zeal was first against Christ, it later became a completely new passion for Christ.

4. Concluding remarks

1. In the light of the above we should wonder whether a Christian encounter with Muslims at the level of spirituality should not have more priority above a dogmatic and apologetic confrontation. This is not meant as a softer approach, as if experiences are always true. Neither is it a pluralistic approach, in which all experiences equal reflections of the Divine. On the contrary, experiences should be open to critique and testing. Nevertheless, religion starts with the heart – with the conviction and experience that faith in God provides an answer to the daily questions and struggles of life.[13] In mission, heart to heart

---

[12] Cf. Reitsma, p. 172.

[13] S.P. Steinhaus, 'The Spirit-first approach to Muslim Evangelism' in: *International Journal of Frontier Mission,* 17/4 (2003), pp. 404-417, explores a focus on the work

encounters are in general much more valuable than dogmatic discussion. The latter tend to start from previously taken positions and rarely convince people of the beauty of Christ. It is important to acknowledge that every spiritual experience, one way or another is related to the presence of the Spirit of God in this world. It expresses respect for and appreciation of the fact that many people are sincerely seeking the one true God and desire to know Him, in order to understand the meaning of life and to find an answer to the fundamental fear of death, pain and suffering. It is especially in a faith encounter that the Spirit is able to reveal the difference between true and surrogate experiences. This requires more of the partners in such a meeting. It is impossible at this level to hide behind dogma's, stereotypes or memorized answers. It is all about integrity: does faith really make a difference in their daily lives or is it an empty box, an emotional drug, or a theoretical and dogmatic truth, that does not really affect them? What does trust in Christ imply when life is getting tough, when disappointments and sorrow, pain and suffering cross our paths? Does it make any difference in our lives that we believe that Christ is the only way, the truth and the life? You will recognize the tree by its fruit (Matt. 7:20); hypocrisy can not remain hidden.

With this approach, we do not abandon fundamental truths. In meeting with Muslims, there will not only be moments of recognition, but also of substantial estrangement. The work of the Spirit is always directed towards Christ, urging people to follow and experience Him. For there is no other name under heaven given among men by which we must be saved.

2. When Muslims pray they pray to God from within their own tradition. Apart from the obligated *Salat*, one of the pillars of Islam, Muslims are also encouraged to pray their own private prayers. Although Muslims might be able to pray several psalms and prayers from the Bible without any problem, it is impossible to pray in Jesus' name, which implies a kind of faith in and commitment to Jesus Christ and his work. Nevertheless, many Muslims can testify to prayers that have been answered: a child might be healed, a job provided, food received. How should we appreciate/regard such answered prayers in the light of the work of the Spirit? Can we say that it is God who answered their prayers, that

---

of the Spirit in opposition to a dogmatic/confessional approach. Although in general a Spirit approach does not in itself contradict a confessional approach, Steinhaus points out that many things that Christians would mention about their faith when meeting Muslims, will easily be cut off or denied, whether it is the Trinity, Jesus the Son of God, or faith in cross and resurrection. Therefore relating to Muslims on a personal level, talking about the Spirit of God or sharing personal stories of faith, can be much more fruitful and rewarding. Apart the personal aspect, Islam is in relating to Christianity much less outspoken in the area of pneumatology than in Christology.

the Spirit was somehow active? Sometimes the only alternative to this response is to attribute the answered prayers to the work of the evil one. Apart from the fact that scripture does not seem to attribute such powers to Satan, it does not allign with the sovereignty of God. For Him to answer prayers is not restricted to only the faithful in Christ, or perfect believers. God does not answer prayers because of the great faith of the believer, or his wonderful words and prayers (cf. Matt. 6:7, 8). It is only God's sovereign grace that is the rationale for answered prayers and that grace is determined by the work of Christ. Therefore it is more plausible/reasonable that those who know Christ and pray in His name, i.e. are connected to what He has done, will pray according to God's will than those who are estranged from him. Still this does not mean that God cannot and does not hear the prayers of those who do not know him in Christ. Otherwise what Paul, quoting the Old Testament, says in Romans 10 would not be true, that "everyone who calls on the name of the Lord will be saved" (Rom. 10:13). For if they need salvation, they are not faithful covenant members and if they have already been saved, they do not need to call upon the Lord. The difference between believers in Christ and others, is that believers are able to recognize answered prayers as God's gift. They will honor and thank Him for that and it will draw them closer to God in Christ. That is the work of the Spirit. Others might not understand their answered prayers as gifts from God and therefore will not acknowledge him and honour him for that. They don't realize that God is at work and attribute their experiences to other forces or influences, which, in turn, occupy their lives. Therefore, as with all spiritual experiences, answered prayers need interpretation and sifting. In order to understand what is from God and what is not, the inspiration of the Holy Spirit is indispensable. In this respect, God's spiritual gifts are not different from all the other gifts He bestows on believers and unbelievers alike, from 'life' as such to health and food.

3. We have argued that, when someone comes to faith in Christ, the experiences from the past are not simply erased or set aside, but will so to speak be regenerated in baptism. Through death, they obtain a new place in a renewed way in the new spiritual experience. That implies that, for these believers there should be space to experience their new faith in the context of their own character, history and culture. They will have to find their own way and form of spiritual life. Acknowledging cultural diversity is also a recognition of the work of the Spirit in religious experiences of non-Christians. However, at the same time, the Spirit also assesses their culture and character in order to transform them. This is very important for the 'insider's movement'-debate.

In this respect, Westerners especially should be restrained. Too often they have confused the work of the Spirit with their own culture and have imposed their experiences arrogantly. Transmission of the gospel often involved conveyance of their own traditions, creeds and dogmas. This is a challenge for

Christians all over the world – to serve God from within and with the aid of their own culture, without compromising the work of the Spirit of Christ.

4. All of this implies that not only other religions are being convicted by the Spirit of Christ in relation to the cross of Christ, but Christianity itself as well. After all, it is not the Christian faith that saves, but Christ. Christians are also human beings that respond to the presence of the Spirit of Christ in the world. They cannot automatically claim that their personal and human experience of the divine is beyond critique, simply because they are Christian. Even Christians are imperfect, hindered by human and cultural limitations and are not completely released from every influence of sin. It is exactly in the confrontation with the spiritual experiences of others that they themselves are being examined and assessed and that blind spots can be revealed – a superb antidote to any form of colonialism in mission.

When it is Christ who saves and not Christianity, we also must emphasize that it is not the Western image of Christ who saves. Of course, we can only know Christ in a specific culture and that is not wrong in itself, as long as we realize that this is not the fullness of Christ. Jesus Christ cannot simply be identified with our image of Him. It is only together with believers from all cultures that we can start to understand who Christ really is. It is only with all the saints that we can comprehend what is the breadth and length and height and depth and to know the love of Christ that surpasses all knowledge, in order that we may be filled with the fullness of God (Eph. 3:18, 19).

5. Because of all of this, we need to make room in our Christian traditions for a variety of faith expressions and experiences. People respond to Gods presence in this world – and to Gods presence in Christ – in very diverse ways. Even within one church, people can experience and express their one faith in Jesus Christ in a wide variety of ways. None of this is disqualified as illegitimate in advance. Not one spiritual experience, from very conservative to extremely charismatical, from evangelical to liturgical can claim to be the one and only unique experience of the Gospel. Therefore a plea for diversity is at the same time a plea for Christian unity. It is my dream that one day sober Calvinists will celebrate God's glory together with exuberant Evangelicals and with Muslim followers of Christ. Only together we can avoid the pitfall of partiality and sectarianism. For whenever we come together in all our diversity, we create a workspace for the Spirit to sharpen and renew us.

CHAPTER 2

Overcoming our Fear of Engagement

Bert de Ruiter

In Europe, with its tens of millions of Muslims there are plenty of opportunities for Evangelical Christians to engage with Muslims through personal contact on a daily basis. Evangelical Christians and Muslims live in the same cities, towns and villages. They share the same apartment blocks; shop in the same shopping centers and market places. They study at the same schools and universities. They travel together on the same buses and in the same metros. They work in the same businesses and offices, relax in the same parks and swimming pools and are members of the same sport clubs. Nevertheless, in spite of all these opportunities for engagement, informal, social interaction between Evangelical Christians and Muslims hardly exists.

In a recently published report *Christianity in its Global Context, 1970-2020: Society, Religion, and Mission*[1], researchers of the Gordon-Conwell's Center for the Study of Global Christianity, found that, in Eastern Europe on average only 17% of Muslims personally know a Christian. Northern Europe, only 16% of Muslims have a Christian friend, whereby friendship does not necessarily refers to a deep or intimate friendship. In Southern Europe, on average 22% of Muslims personally know a Christian in a more than casual or superficial way. In Western Europe only 19% of Muslims have significant contact with Christians.

In their report, they define 'Christians' as "followers of Jesus Christ of all kinds, all traditions and confessions, and all degrees of commitment." Evangelicals, as a subset of all Christians, would therefore most likely have an even lower rate of contact with Muslims. This means that only a small minority of Evangelical Christians in Europe has an ongoing meaningful relationship with Muslims.

The relationship between Evangelicals and Muslims in Europe can be described with the same words the Apostle John used to describe the relationship between the Jews and the Samaritans in Jesus' time, namely: "Jews do not associate with Samaritans." (John 4:10).

---

[1] Report *Christianity in its Global Context, 1970-2020: Society, Religion, and Mission*, researchers of the Gordon-Conwell's Center for the Study of Global Christianity.Todd M. Johnson and Charles L. Tieszen, "Personal Contact: The *sine qua non* of Twenty-first Century Christian Mission," *Evangelical Missions Quarterly*, October 2007, pp. 494-502.

What is it that hinders Evangelical Christians from developing meaningful relationships with their Muslim neigbours? Why do so many Evangelicals in Europe find it easier to pray for missionaries in Muslim countries than to say 'good morning' to the Muslim that crosses their path or that sits next to them in a bus? Why do many Evangelicals talk *about* Islam among one another in stead of *with* Muslims? Why do so many Evangelicals rather buy a book about Muslims than use that money to buy a cup of coffee for their Muslim neighbor and ask him or her about their life and beliefs?

I have come to the conclusion that the biggest factor preventing Evangelicals from establishing meaningful relations with Muslims is their fear of and prejudice towards Muslims. This in itself is not surprising, because they live in societies in which a negative attitude towards Muslims is widespread.

In her book *Why the West Fears Islam*, Jocelyne Cesari writes:

"A review of the most significant public opinion polls and surveys among European … citizens conducted in the past decade confirms the widespread negative feelings towards Muslims and Islam as expressed by politicians."[2]

She points out that *"the sentiment that clearly comes across is a broadly felt discomfort with Islam and a widespread association of Islam and Muslims as a force of unwanted, and potentially irreversible, change."*[3]

She identifies four trends that lay behind these feelings:

1. Muslims have not and will not integrate.
2. Muslims are a threat to national identity now and in the future.
3. Public practices, such as mosque-building, prayer, and clothing should be kept to a minimum.
4. Islam and Muslims are incompatible with national and Western values.[4]

She concludes: *"A common point across surveys is that non-Muslims mostly fear that the presence of Muslims will affect their way of life or alter the norms of an assumed mainstream. In other words, while non-Muslims may nor have a direct problem with Muslims or individual Muslims, they fear that Muslims – particularly growing numbers of them – will impose unwanted changes in their countries."*[5]

---

[2] Jocelyne Cesari, *Why the West Fears Islam: An Exploration of Muslims in Liberal Democracies* (New York, Palgrave MacMilland, 2013), p. 13.

[3] Ibid., p. 14.

[4] Ibid., p. 14.

[5] Ibid., p. 15.

Many Evangelicals share these convictions with their unbelieving fellow Europeans. In fact, some give additional reasons for their fear and anxiety.

Quite a few Evangelicals point out that Islam is spread by the sword. They argue that Muslims invaded Europe in the seventh century AD and expanded into the heartlands of Christianity, where, after Islam arrived on the scene, the church that previously blossomed was persecuted with the result that "sections of the church have disappeared completely in the face of the challenge of Islam."[6]

Others draw attention to the military campaigns of the Ottoman Empire in the fifteenth century, which led to various degrees of Islamisation in their conquered Eastern European regions.

Serbian Orthodox professor Trifkovic expresses what I have heard many Christians say to me when we talk about Islam: *"Islam is and always has been a religion of intolerance, a jihad without an end. ... Islam was spread by the sword and has been maintained by the sword throughout its history."*[7]

Some Christians justify their fear and prejudice of Muslims because they are convinced that the use of violence goes back to the very heart and origin of Islam, namely to the Qur'an and the example of Muhammad.

"Islam, in Muhammad's texts and its codification, discriminates against us. It is extremely offensive. Those who submit to that faith must solve the problem they set themselves. Islam discriminates against all "unbelievers.""[8]

The Arab-Israeli conflict also influences the way Christians in Europe look at Islam. Many Evangelicals believe that because of Islam, there are troubles in Israel. Many Christians, especially Evangelicals, back the State of Israel, claiming that its establishment in 1948 fulfills biblical prophecies and they believe the Christian community should oppose those who hate Israel, such as Muslims.

The growing persecution of Christians in some Islamic countries also triggers fear and anxiety among Evangelicals in Europe.

Another kind of fear expressed among Christians is the fear of losing one's personal space or territory. Some look at the demographics of Islam in Europe and are fearful that Europe will become Muslim in the near future. David Pawson, a prominent contemporary Bible teacher and worldwide speaker based in

---

[6] Patrick Sookhdeo, *Islam: the Challenge to the Church* (Wiltshire, UK: Isaac Publishing, 2006), p. 2.

[7] Serge Trifkovic, *The Sword of the Prophet: Islam, history, theology, impact on the world* (Boston: Regina Orthodox Press, Inc. 2002), p. 132.

[8] Trifkovic, p. 301.

Great Britain, believes that he has received a prophetic revelation from God that Islam will take over England.[9]

The reasons given for one's fear and anxiety towards Muslims in Europe are understandable. Violence does take place in name of Islam. There are intolerant verses in the Qur'an. Christians are being persecuted in many Islamic countries. There are Muslims in Europe seeking to overthrow our governments to establish a Caliphat.

On the other hand, we do well to realize that overwhelming majority of Muslims refrain from using violence, that most Muslim scholars interpret the violent verses in the Qu'ran is a less strict way, and that Christians also face persecution from other Christians or from secular governments. Nevertheless, this does not take away the predominantly negative attitude towards Islam and Muslims prevalent in Europe, and that has also affected evangelical churches.

I believe that this negative attitude is one of the key reasons why Evangelicals in Europe are reluctant to engage with Muslims through personal contact and friendship.

Many of those involved in evangelizing Muslims, rely heavily on non-personal methods of evangelism (e.g. use of DVD, literature distribution, chatrooms on internet). There is nothing wrong with the use of good, culturally appropriate and timely media, to share the Gospel with Muslims, as long as we realize that media are extensions of the human body.

The microphone becomes an extension of the voice, the pencil an extension of the hand, and the camera an extension of the eye. In Christian communication we are channels through which the gospel of Jesus Christ is extended to others, and we use media to extend ourselves and our message to others.[10]

Non-personal methods of evangelism and mission might help us to overcome barriers, or to provide extra information to those we a reaching with the Gospel or discipling in the Christian faith, but we cannot depend on these at the expense of personal contact.

It is important for us to realize that the most important channels that God wants to use to communicate the Gospel to Muslims in Europe are His children, disciples of Jesus Christ, who share their lives and the Gospel with Muslims.

---

[9] David Pawson, *The Challenge of Islam to Christians* (London: Hodder & Stoughton, 2003).
[10] Viggo Sogaard, *Media in Church and Mission: communicating the Gospel* (Pasadena, California, William Carey Library, 1993), p. 39.

The "Word became flesh" (John 1:14), referring to the incarnation of Jesus is the model par excellence for the ministry of Christians in Europe towards Muslims. The incarnation is the ideal model of communication

The final and complete communication of God to humanity was in the form of a human body: the incarnation of Jesus Christ. In Christ the message and the medium became one. Acceptance of the Person is the beginning point of change, and central to that is the question of trust. What gives communication its character is not only the message but the messenger. A cassette tape is listened to a video is watched, because it is brought there by someone who is trusted.[11]

Communication through incarnation is being involved with the people we are dealing with in their context, entering into their real problems, issues, and struggles. *"Jesus did not just speak to the Jews, but he became a Jew and identified himself with all aspects of Jewish life. He identified with the social outcasts, and participated in the social relationships of the Jewish culture. He became a true human being, even working as a carpenter. He spoke to their particular needs, rather than presenting a message of universal abstracts."*[12]

Like Jesus, we must dwell among the people we wish to call to faith in Him. When we engage with Muslims through "incarnational evangelism," we personally incarnate the Gospel among them.

This model was also one of the Apostle Paul's ways of witnessing about Jesus Christ. He writes about this in his letter to the church in Thessalonica: *"Because we loved you so much, we were delighted to share with you not only the gospel of God, but our lives as well." (1 Thess. 2:8, NIV)*

Paul's Epistle to the Thessalonians was his earliest epistle written during his second missionary journey around AD 52. Paul and Silas had preached the gospel in Thessalonica less than a year previously. They had to leave Thessalonica before they completed their work due to the great opposition to the Gospel by the Jews. While in Athens, Timothy brought Paul word from the church in Thessalonica (1 Thess. 3:6), together with questions that they had raised. Paul wrote his first epistle in response to their overture.

In chapter one, Paul begins with a greeting followed by thanksgiving for the work of God and the response of the Thessalonians to the Gospel. In chapter two, Paul gives a review of his ministry to the Thessalonians (2:1-12). In light of the slander Paul had received from the religious Judaizers who claimed he was only out for personal gain, Paul reviews his and his team's ministry and emphasizes their motives and conduct. Paul refers to his own character and manner of living for proof of what he was saying to the Thessalonians.

---

[11] Ibid., p. 96.
[12] Ibid., pp. 14-15.

He emphasizes his and his coworkers' boldness in proclaiming the Gospel in the face of opposition (1-2), the purity of their motives and actions (3-6), their friendly and loving attitude (7-8), and their holy, righteous, and blameless behavior (10-12).

Nine times in this letter Paul writes "you know..." referring to the Thessalonians' firsthand knowledge of Paul's life. Paul's emphasis on motives and conduct in the midst of proclaiming the gospel makes clear that the manner in which one proclaims the gospel and the character of the messengers needs to be in harmony with the content of the gospel. In his commentary on 1 Thessalonians, J. Vernon McGee believes that Paul's exemplified in Thessalonica that the greatest sermon one will ever preach is by the life that one lives:

If you were asked to choose, what would you select as the greatest sermon of the apostle Paul ...? I would choose his life in Thessalonica. His greatest sermon was not in writing or speaking, but in walking. It was not in exposition, but in experience; not in his profession, but in his practice. He took his text from James 2:26, faith without works is dead and he made his points on the pavement of the streets of Thessalonica.[13]

In verse eight Paul points out that he and his team had a genuine love for the people they shared the Gospel with. They not only delivered a message, but also gave themselves. In his commentary on this verse, scholar F.F. Bruce writes that "to share their own lives involved utter self-denial, spending and being spent in the interest of others." He also points out that the word used for *life* here is *Psuche*, which is the seat of affection and will and concludes that "the meaning is not simply we were willing to give (lay down) our lives for you but we were willing to give ourselves to you, to put ourselves at your disposal, without reservation."[14]

In his commentary, Ernest Best applies Paul's example to all missionaries when he writes that "the true missionary is not someone specialized in the delivery of the message but someone who's whole being, completely committed to a message which demands all, is communicated to his hearers."[15]

---

[13] J. Vernon McGee, *1 & 2 Thessalonians (Through the Bible commentary series)* (Nashville, Tennessee: Thomas Nelson, Inc, 1995), pp. 35ff; quoted in http://www.preceptaustin.org/1thessalonians_21-htm (January 24, 2009).

[14] F.F. Bruce, *1 and 2 Thessalonians*, ed. Bruce M. Metzger, *Word Biblical Commentary* (Dallas: Word Incorporated, 1982), pp. 23ff.

[15] Ernest Best, *Black's New Testament Commentaries*, ed., *A commentary of the First and Second Epistles to the Thessalonians* (Peabody, Massachusetts: Hendrickson Publishers, 1993), pp. 102-103.

Applying the truth of this verse to evangelism among Muslims, three things stand out: (1) Evangelism is a lifestyle, not just an activity. Verbal sharing of the Gospel needs to be integrated in one's life and linked with addressing social needs that are a result of a broken relationship with the Lord; (2) In order for Muslims to have an accurate understanding of Jesus Christ and the biblical faith, they need to see an expression of it in the lives of people they know and trust;[16] (3) Christians who want to incarnate the truth of the Gospel to Muslims need to have an accurate understanding of Muslims in the context of a relationship of love and trust. Loving and understanding the people who need the Gospel is vital for sharing the Gospel with them. All three aspects mean that there needs to be close proximity between Christians and Muslims, or to put it differently, Christians need to share their lives with Muslims.

For Evangelicals in Europe to follow Paul's example in Thessalonica in our dealings with Muslims, we must overcome fear and anxiety. Our fear, anxiety and prejudice represent a barrier for personal contact, healthy dialogue and mutual understanding with Muslims. How will Muslims see Christ living in us when we isolate ourselves from their social, ethnic and cultural groups? How can Evangelicals in Europe overcome their fear of engagement with Muslims that has led to this severe lack of personal contact? How can we overcome our fear to interact with Muslims on a regular basis?

Let me suggest five stepping stones, that can be easily remembered through the acronymn of the word 'Grace':

1. God is sovereign
2. Rejoice in the grace of God in your life
3. Accept that Islam is what a Muslim says it is
4. Contact real Muslims
5. Enter into their lives

---

[16] J. Dudley Woodberry, G. Shubin, and G. Marks, "Why Muslims Follow Jesus," *Christianity Today*, October 24, 2007. Dr. Woodberry, professor of Islamic Studies at Fuller, researched what attracts Muslims to follow Jesus. Between 1991 and 2007 about 750 Muslims who have decided to follow Christ filled out an extensive questionnaire. The number one reason respondents – from 30 countries and 50 ethnic groups – representing every major region of the Muslim world, listed, for their decision to follow Christ was the lifestyle of the Christians among them.

God is sovereign

Our fear and anxiety regarding Islam and Muslims in Europe can cause us to loose sight of the sovereignty of God. Fear often distorts our sense of reality. It distorts the size of our problems, or the strength of those we believe to be our enemies, so that they seem huge and undefeatable. But perhaps most significantly, fear distorts our picture of God. God seems weak, uninvolved, or uncaring in the midst of our troubles. This was the situation of the people of God in the time of Isaiah. They were disappointed in God, believing God didn't see, He didn't know and didn't care. They said to each other: "My way is hidden from the Lord, my cause is disregarded by my God" (Isaiah 40:27) and also "The Lord has forsaken me, the Lord has forgotten me." (Isaiah 49:14). They were discouraged, depressed, insecure and afraid.

In this dark period of Israel's history, God called the prophet Isaiah to comfort His people and in doing so, he regularly tells them not to fear (eg. 40:9; 41:10, 13, 14; 43:1, 5; 44:2, 8; 51:7, 12; 54:4, 14). God wants to help His people overcome their fear, by pointing them to Himself: "do not be afraid; say ... Here is your God." (Isaiah 40:9). God comforts his fearful people by revealing more of Himself: *"I, even I, am he who comforts you. Who are you that you fear mere mortals, human beings who are but grass, that you forget the Lord your Maker, who stretches out the heavens and who lays the foundations of the earth, that you live in constant terror every day ...."* (Isaiah 51:12, 13)

In His sovereignty, God has allowed millions of Muslims to come and live and settle and grow in our continent – which has become their continent. Most of all, Europe is God's continent. He rules over schemes and evil plots of man. He will care for His people. He will build His Church. Learning to trust His sovereignty helps us to deal with our fears of Muslims.

Rejoice in God's grace

C.S. Lewis once said that Christianity's unique feature among world religions is grace. Studying the concept of grace, we find it runs through the whole Bible. God is called the God of all grace, who sits on the throne of grace. He has sent out His Spirit of grace, who equips Christians to proclaim the Gospel of grace, which is about Jesus, who is the ultimate manifestation of God's grace. Because of importance of grace in all that God is and does, it is something that should be seen in the lives of those who call Him their Father.

Receiving grace from God in daily abundance is meant to transform our beings and guide all our actions. Nevertheless, Christians are not always known for their grace.

"The two major causes of most emotional problems among evangelical Christians are the failure to understand, receive, and live out God's unconditional

grace and forgiveness, and the failure to give out that unconditional love, forgiveness, and grace to other people ... We read, we hear, we believe a good theology of grace. But that's not the way we live. The good news of the Gospel of grace has not penetrated the level of our emotions."[17]

We are called to respond to Muslims with grace.

Steve Bell defines a grace-response as follows:

A grace-response is ... "a willingness to alter the default mechanism in our brains which causes us to fear the unfamiliar in another person; being prepared to give others the benefit of the doubt and make an effort to find out why they behave as they do."[18]

The more we learn to rejoice in God's grace for us, the more we begin to understand that God is also gracious to others around us – and the more we will become channels of that grace, also to Muslims around us.

Accept that Islam is what a Muslim says it is

Fear and prejudice are often based on stereotypes, which come from a closed view of Islam that considers Islam in Europe as a monolithic bloc, and fundamentalist Muslims are made representative of the whole of Islam. On the other hand, an open view of Islam emphasizes the social, linguistic, national, ethnic and religious differences among Muslims.

Stereotypes (labels) depersonalize individuals. We should be careful to ascribe to all Muslims opinions or behaviors that are characteristic of a small number of Muslims. It is important to differentiate between 'abstract' Islam and 'live' Islam. We never meet Islam, we only meet Muslims and their Islam.

I think that in order to understand what Islam is, one has to stop talking about a single Islam as a stereotype. Think of a palette on which painters put all the colours they are going to use – I would suggest that Islam, like Christianity ... has many different colours on its palette.[19]

It is important to understand that Islam is not a monolithic entity. It is impossible to speak of Islam in Europe (singular) as if millions of Muslims believe the same, behave the same, think the same, interpret the Qur'an the same, pray the same or relate to others the same. Essentially, Islam is what a Muslim says it is.

---

[17] David A. Seamands, *Healing for Damaged Emotions*, (Scripture Press, Victory Books, USA, 1991), p. 32.

[18] Steve Bell, *Grace for Muslim? The journey from fear to faith*, (Milton Keynes: Authentic Media, 2006), p. 1.

[19] Tariq Ali, "Why are we so obsessed by Islam?" in *Islam and Europe – Challenges and Opportunities* Marie-Claire Foblets (ed); Leuven University Press, 2008, p. 164.

Contact real Muslims

Once we have regained our trust in the sovereignty of God and have learned to rejoice in God's grace for us and thus begin to view Muslims as human beings with a particular faith, not as representatives of a religious system, we might be ready to actually contact real Muslims. Fear and prejudice towards Islam and Muslims are often strongest in those who have little if any personal contact with Muslims. Fear makes us to withdraw in our own circles, instead of crossing a bridge (or a street) toward Muslims.

When God opens our hearts and eyes, we don't just see a 'veil', but we see Samira, a mother, who seeks to raise her children in a strange and often hostile environment. We don't just see a Muslim, but we see Hassan, a hardworking father who wonders whether his body will last until his retirement. We don't see 'a Muslim immigrant', but we see Hossaine and Khadija, a young man and a young woman, who have great hopes about their future, but wonder whether they can find a suitable job. We might even begin to see the fears and anger behind the facade of Samir, a Muslim extremist.

Enter into the lives of Muslims

We are called to be witnesses of Christ. Our initial contact with Muslims might lead to a deepening relationship in which we will have opportunities to share our faith. We've seen that the Apostle Paul often integrated sharing the Gospel with sharing his life with people. When we do so, Muslims will see what we believe and how this affects our behavior.

"What makes us different is not simply what we believe, but how our beliefs motivate and affect our behavior. What makes us different is how our faith transforms the way we live ... Unless we ... learn to demonstrate that dynamic and transforming relationship between our beliefs and our behavior we are in no better position than any other faith "[20]

Witnessing of our faith to Muslims should ideally be incorporated in a relationship of love, trust and respect. It takes time to develop such a relationship, going far beyond a one-time discussion with a stranger about the Christian faith and Islam. Among other things, it means doing things together, spending time together, developing interest in each other's life, sharing our joys and grief, becoming good friends in the full sense of the word. It means sharing your whole life, not just sharing the Gospel.

Our sincere concern and care, provides us with plenty opportunities to share Biblical truths – not in an abstract way void of relational connection, but as

---

[20] Richard Sudworth, *Distinctly Welcoming*, (NSW Australia: Scripture Union Australia, 2007), p. 48.

part of our daily life. In natural everyday scenes, your can live out your faith before your Muslim friends in word and in deed. There will be exchanges in conversation where you will express Christian truths or pray with or for your friend. They will see you practicing your faith (e.g. fasting, celebrating Christmas, how you deal with conflict, how you handle money, how you relate to your family). Our Muslim friends will observe in daily living the saving work and power of Jesus. Most Muslims come to a true appreciation of the gospel and desire for our Lord by seeing the Christian faith lived out in the daily struggles of real Christians, serving openly, humbly, faithfully, by their side, in their communities.

Sometimes confrontation may occur as difficult questions are asked but, as friends, we know how to disagree in appropriately. Incarnational witness can be costly and painful, as we see in Jesus' life of suffering and even death.

How often you are able to share about the Gospel cannot be programmed. Out of concern for people who have not heard about Christ, you will be praying for God to help you see when to speak, when to listen, and how to be sensitive to your friend's needs and beliefs. Also, you will learn to become more outspoken about your own faith and become more explicit in pointing out how God relates to the choices you make and the responses you give.

In the Bible, we read about Andrew bringing his brother Peter to meet Jesus, and Philip bringing his friend Nathanael to Jesus. Evangelism is described as bringing our friends to meet our best Friend: Jesus. As relational witnesses, we want to have our Muslim friends meet Jesus, our best Friend, so that they bow to His Lordship and come his friend, too.

Conclusion

The presence of Muslims in our towns and streets might affect our way of life and might bring about changes in our societies. But is this something we should fight against or learn to adapt to?

Our identity is not wrapped up with our national citizenship or being European. Our identity is found in our relationship with God – in being reconciled, forgiven, accepted and adopted.

This identity is secure and untouchable, in the hands of a sovereign God, who has become our Heavenly Father. He can be trusted to fulfill His promises. As people whose citizenship is in heaven, we are supposed to be aliens and strangers in Europe. We are called to fear God, not circumstances, changes, nor even people. Fearing God means, among other things, to allow Him to be the judge, to allow Him to craft the future for Europe, to allow Him to give and to take freedom, welfare and security. Trusting in the sovereign God creates space in our hearts for His love, compassion, kindness, hospitality for our Muslim neighbors. Through the empowerment of the Spirit, Christians can become trendsetters, not trend followers.

Wouldn't it be great when each Muslim in Europe had at least one Christian friend who loves them enough to share their life, who is interested in them, who is willing to treat them as a person and not as a potential terrorist, a friend who shows them what Christ is able to do in lives that are submitted to Him? Will you be such a friend?

CHAPTER 3

The Socio-political Context of Our Engagement

Efan Elias

1. Introduction

The world of missions to Muslims, or any other group is never removed from the economic, cultural and political context that it works within. For that reason, it is useful to spend a chapter exploring the wider context within which missionaries seeking to evangelise Muslims in Europe will be working. Other chapters will engage with the trends, dynamics and movements within European Muslim communities themselves. For this chapter, the focus will be upon the wider European cultural, political and legal contexts.

In order to control the scope of the discussion, the chapter will look at the place of religion at an EU level, rather than at national levels. In many ways, the workings of high politics and diplomacy seem far removed from the everyday human engagements which form an integral part of missions work. Hopefully, this chapter will help us to understand that the opinions, laws and directives coming from EU's institutions provide an important backdrop for mission workers anywhere in Europe.

2. Historical and Cultural Portrait

Every commentator, academic, journalist and politician with even a limited interest in religious affairs in Europe will argue that religion in Europe, especially Christianity, is in long-term decline toward eventual extinction. Figures across all western European states appear to confirm the grinding, inexorable rise of atheism (10-15% over the last decade) at the expense of all religions. This broadly consistent dynamic was confirmed in a recent (2010) *Eurobarometer* poll, which found that 54% of Europeans claimed to believe in a god. A further 25% believed in some form of spirit world and 21% described themselves as atheist.

Europe, then appears to be moving away from religious affiliation. However, this generalisation does mask some 'anomalies' from different parts of the EU. For example, the Anglican diocese of Nottingham in the UK reports a 16% increase in weekly church attendance over 2010-2011. From a very low postwar population of around 50,000, twenty years ago, French evangelicals are now estimated to number between 450,000 and 500,000.[1] Furthermore, the

---

[1] *The Guardian*, 'Comment is Free', 6th November 2009.

recent UK census (2011), which included a section on religion, revealed that London was experiencing an overall increase in the number of Christians. University of London scholar Eric Kaufmann, having tracked religious data in the UK over more than two decades, argued that the way that London goes religiously, the rest of the UK follows.[2]

Whatever the truth behind the statistics, the perception of policymakers in Brussels and in capitals across the EU is that religion is, broadly speaking, an issue of declining importance. As such, their engagement with religion in general is on broad questions of integration, terrorism and cohesion. That said, there is an acknowledgement that, until religion dies out completely, religious communities will need to be engaged with. The EU has set-out to do so against a backdrop of long-standing concern to ensure that, whilst religion maybe in its death throes, it must not claw its way back into the public space.

Church-State Relations in Europe have frequently been shaped by the conflicts over the limits of sovereign power from the Medieval period through to the Reformation and Enlightenment times. Much of the conflict has revolved around the extent to which the Church should have control over naturally pastoral areas of public life such as education, welfare and health. From the Church's point of view, such areas were the natural purview of its role in society. Yet the fact that priests, bishops, abbots, friars, monks and nuns were answerable to the Popes and Cardinals, rather than the secular rulers, was an ongoing source of frustration to secular authorities. As monarchs and fresh republican authorities rebelled against Catholic authority and began to take over these pastoral areas, the church was pushed into private life. In-so-doing, secular rulers were able to have complete authority over the whole of their realms, rather than the limited sovereignty they had exercised before. The long-term scars that this conflict has left on secular authorities have impacted the psyche of government officials across Europe to this day.

Thus, in coming to our central discussion about religion, evangelism, freedom of religion or belief, or blasphemy as it effects mission work, it is important to remember that EU officials, like their counterparts in national governments across the member states, are very wary of religion somehow seeking a way back into the public space. Furthermore, it is worthwhile acknowledging that, with the advent mass immigration over the last sixty years or so, Hinduism and Islam have become part of that dynamic. Indeed, there are many reasons to believe that Islam has taken over the church as the key interlocutor for navigating Church-state relations on the continent.

---

[2] See http://www.lapidomedia.com/census-analysis-busy-believers-belie-statistics-doom (15th March 2014).

3. Current Issues

3.1 The regard for religion

Broadly speaking, active participation by religions at official levels, within the EU fabric, was enshrined in the EU's constitution signed at Lisbon in 2004. There had been much debate over the extent to which there should be an acknowledgement of Christianity's contribution to European history in the constitution. In the end, no acknowledgement was made, despite strong representation from Germany especially. However, Article 17 enshrined a 'consultative role' for all official religions in the EU and, moreover, committed the Commission to meeting with religious leaders at least once a year. These meetings had been going on informally already, but Article 17 ensured that the process would be a committment.[3] One might argue that this process encapsulates the EU approach to religion in general, as has been described above, for it allows religion no special place; it effectively reduces its status to that of any other advocacy group. On the other hand, it has fixed a regular opportunity for EU officials to take the temperature of the religious caucus across the member states. Religion thus has an officially acknowledged 'consultative role', but it also has informal routes of influence within the institutional apparatus. There are a number of Catholics within the EU Parliament and Commission which, coupled with the ongoing Papal support of what they call 'the European Project', has enabled the Roman Catholic church to bring informal influence to bear. That is seen most clearly in the EU's statements on Christian persecution around the world – an issue brought to prominence in the EU through the work of the Catholics especially within the Parliament, as well as through the lobbying of COMECE.[4]

The Commission has allowed religious engagement in areas with a specifically religious element, such as FoRB, but has sought to limit the role played in the political and policy life of the EU through creating a consultative relationship. Against this background, the changing ethno-cultural life of the EU has further muddied the waters of EU-religious relations. Since the end of the Second World War, secular philosophy has dominated policymaking at the same time as western European states have gone into a period of post-colonial self-questioning, which dynamics became the basis of the multiculturalism move-

---

[3] The dialogue agenda and administration comes under the purview of BEPA and their website on the dialogue process can be found here http://ec.europa.eu/bepa/activities/outreach-team/dialogue/index_en.htm (31st March 2014).

[4] A link to the COMECE web-page on Religious Freedom can be found here http://www.comece.eu/site/en/activities/policyareas/fundamentalrights/religiousfreedom (31st March 2014).

ment that welcomed the beliefs and philosophies of growing immigrant populations. This uncritical openness to new ideas, coupled with the shear accumulated mass of immigrant numbers, has begun to begin to fundamentally shift traditional European culture and helped fuel the rise of the political right, exacerbated by the competition for jobs and benefits during the harsh economic climate that has prevailed since 2008 across the continent. This has resulted in the specifically anti-Muslim stance taken by some nationalist parties such as the British National Party as Muslim political activism has, in many peoples' minds, come to epitomise the impact of immigration.

On one level, this targeting of Islam is unsurprising given the visibility of Muslim activism and concerns over terrorism. Yet, these concerns about the impact of immigration – coupled with the apparent growth of Muslim minorities and the search for desperately needed money by european governments – has produced an equal and opposite effect on the continent. Shari'a finance has begun to boom, with all the major financial centres in Europe beginning to develop a far greater usage of shari'a compliant instruments.[5] On the other hand, countries such as France, Italy and Belgium have also adopted bans on Islamic dress covering the full body.[6] Muslims have been vociferous in their denunciation of cartoons seen as insulting to Muhammad, and a long campaign over the balance of free speech against 'defamation' continues to be fought.[7] Tied into the same dynamic are questions concerning the application of blasphemy laws, which continue to be on the statute books in Cyprus, the Czech Republic, Denmark, Spain (where the artist Javier Krahe was recently arrested under blasphemy laws for insulting the Catholic Church), Finland, Germany, Greece, Italy, Lithuania, the Netherlands, Poland, Portugal and Slovakia.[8] Indeed, in the UK, which abolished its blasphemy law in 2008, groups such as ENGAGE (Muslim advocacy group) are campaigning hard for a change to blasphemy laws.[9] To that end, the Organisation of the Islamic Conference (OIC) has been working hard at the UN level to ensure that religious sensibili-

---

[5] See Richard Partington's article 'Deutsche Bank predicts Islamic Finance boom.' at http://www.efinancialnews.com/story/2011-11-15/deutsche-bank-analysts-predict-islamic-finance-boom?ea9c8a2de0ee111045601ab04d673622 (1st April 2014).

[6] Interesting discussion on challenges to these laws at http://america.aljazeera.com/articles/2013/11/27/france-defends-fullfaceveilbanateuropeanrightscourt.html (31st March 2014).

[7] A fascinating selection of opinions is contained in David Hayes and Tony Curzon Price's 'Europe and Islam: Controversy, Protest and Dialogue'. *Open Democracy Quarterly* Series 1 Vol. 1, January 2007. pp. 53-110.

[8] See Norman Doe, *Comparative Religion in Europe*. Oxford: OUP, 2013. p. 142.

[9] ENGAGE hosted a British Parliamentary Exhibition on 'Islamophobia Awareness Month' in 2013 as part of their campaign for blasphemy laws in the UK.

ties will be 'respected'. This advocacy has been rewarded with the recent passing of the Human Rights Council Resolution 16/18 on 'defamation'.[10] Muslims have become the most visible incarnation of the changes that many Europeans fear on the continent.

The struggle around the rights of the religious groups in relation to other human rights involves more than just Islam. The cases of Lillian Ladele, Nadia Eweida, Shirley Chaplin and Gary McFarlane – in which equalities legislation has apparently trumped the personal convictions of the believer – are the most high profile examples of increasing Christian alienation from European culture.[11]

These cases highlight that the historic desire to preserve the secular public space is very much alive today. The only difference is the change in the ethno-cultural makeup of the continent, which has added Islam, Hinduism and Buddhism to what was once a two-way fight. What is also new is that Islam particularly has an expectation of church-state fusion entirely at odds with the prevailing culture of the continent. Christianity has no such expectation, although historically there had been such a fusion. Thus it has been able to adapt to its more uncomfortable situation on the continent.

3.2 Freedom of Religion or Belief (FoRB)

Having looked at the current situation of religion in general within the EU, what is the situation of FoRB itself on the continent and why is there such a lack of clarity concerning its parameters? Some of this has been touched upon in the previous section when we have briefly highlighted the situation of Muslim and Christian activism around equalities legislation, but it is important to look at what the EU itself as a body sees as its duties in this area.

On the 28th April, 2013 the European Parliamentary Assembly called on 'member States to accommodate religious beliefs in the public sphere by guaranteeing freedom of thought in relation to health care, education and the civil service.' With the caveat that "the rights of others to be free from discrimination

---

[10] Both the US and EU are participating actively in the process which is the outworking of HRC Resolution 16/18. The EU's engagement with the process is detailed at http://eeas.europa.eu/delegations/un_geneva/press_corner/all_news/news/2013/20130619_oic_hrc_event_en.htm (31st March 2014).

[11] An interesting report on the cases by Jamie Grierson 'European Court of Human Rights rejects Christians' cases that their religious rights were violated by employers.' http://www.independent.co.uk/news/uk/home-news/european-court-of-human-rights-rejects-christians-cases-that-their-religious-rights-were-violated-by-employers-8634687.html (24th March 2014).

are respected and that the access to lawful services is guaranteed." The measure was adopted almost unanimously, by a vote of 148-3, with 7 abstentions.[12]

This Resolution typified the EU's approach to questions of FoRB: displayed a desire to be committed to FoRB, but did little to clarify the processes of ensuring the preservation of those rights beyond passing the issue to national governments. For an institution that has consistently been accused of trying to increase its federal reach, this was a somewhat surprising move and it brings into sharp relief the extent to which the EU does not really want to get involved in these issues internally – somewhat ironic given the EU's strong stance on FoRB issues internationally.[13]

On the face of it, the EU has had a long and distinguished history in ensuring the religious liberty of its citizens and pushing for those same rights in non-EU countries. In the early days of the EC, as it was then, Article 9 of the European Convention on Human Rights (ECHR1) Rome, 1950 specified that "Everyone has the right to freedom of thought, conscience and religion; this right includes freedom to change his religion or belief and freedom, either alone or in community with others and in public or private, to manifest his religion or belief, in worship, teaching, practice and observance." Part Two of the same article proclaimed that "Freedom to manifest one's religion or beliefs shall be subject only to such limitations as are prescribed by law and are necessary in a democratic society in the interests of public safety, for the protection of public order, health or morals, or for the protect of the rights and freedoms of others." These principals were re-affirmed in Article 9 of the Convention for the Protection of Human Rights and Fundamental Freedoms (CPHRFF) when the EP met in Strasbourg in 2010.[14]

However, between 1950 and 2010, the Charter of Fundamental Rights of the European Union (CFREU) was passed in Brussels in 2000 wherein Article 10 of that document said that "Everyone has the right to freedom of thought, conscience and religion. This right includes freedom to change religion or belief and freedom, either alone or in community with others and in public or in private, to manifest religion or belief, in worship, teaching, practice and observance." On the face of it, this first element of the article was fully in line with the documents mentioned above, but the second part shifted the ground a little, saying that "The right to conscientious objection is recognised, in ac-

---

[12] It is Resolution 1928 of the Parliamentary Assembly of the Council of Europe.

[13] See Sean Oliver-Dee 'The European Union's engagement with issues of religious freedom' *Journal of Faith in International Affairs*. Autumn 2014 (forthcoming).

[14] A full copy of the text can be found at http://conventions.coe.int/treaty/en/treaties/html/005.htm (24th March 2014).

cordance with the national laws governing the exercise of this right."[15] In essence therefore, rather than talking in general terms of FoRB being framed by "only such limitations as are prescribed by law and are necessary in a democratic society in the interests of public safety" as had been specified in 1950 and 2010, the CFREU hit the the question of determining the extent of FoRB into national spheres, thereby negating EU's need to deal with the question internally other than through the ECHR. That is not to say that the EU is entirely removed from engaging with FoRB issues internally. For example, in January 2013 a new EU directive allowing for ritual slaughter, including *halal*, came into effect. In many ways this seems a random engagement with FoRB issues within the EU as it has not waded into much bigger issues of the day such as the Islamic body coverings that were mentioned earlier. Indeed, this EU-wide directive has brought an instant response from some national governments (such as Poland) and appears to have opened the door to complex legal argument for some time to come.[16]

In many ways, it would seem that this move would make it harder for religious minorities, including Christianity, to know where they stand in relation to a whole range of FoRB issues whether in the workplace or in education such as in the examples cited earlier. But what seems retrograde on one level has actually had some material benefits in other ways. Indeed, the EU legislation has forced a number of European states which had previously sought to ban it to open themselves up once again to allow it. For example, the right to proselytise has been recognised by the Constitutional Court in Spain since May 2000.[17] Six years later, the Parliamentary Constitutional Committee in Finland also recognised the right to proselytise.[18] However, that is not to say that the right to proselytise has been universally adopted throughout the EU; it is still forbidden in Greece.[19] Many states are cautious about allowing proselytisation without any caveats as in Cyprus, which forbids proselytisation if it includes any form of coercion.[20] This

---

[15] A full copy of the text of that document can be found here http://www.europarl.europa.eu/charter/pdf/text_en.pdf (24th March 2014).

[16] An EU parliamentary briefing about ritual slaughter can be found at http://www.europarl.europa.eu/RegData/bibliotheque/briefing/2012/120375/LDM_BRI(2012)120375_REV2_EN.pdf and an article about Poland's objections to the ritual slaughter case can be found at http://www.bbc.co.uk/news/world-europe-20523809. More recently the Danish authorities have also moved to ban religious slaughter and an article about that can be found at http://europenews.dk/en/node/77059. All these articles were accessed on 24th March 2014.

[17] Judgement 141/2000.

[18] Report 17/2006.

[19] Greek Constitution, Article 18.2.

[20] Cypriot Constitution Article 18.5.

seems entirely reasonable and would be widely welcomed by evangelists themselves. However the definition of 'coercion' itself is not clearly understood likely, further legal cases will be needed in order to pin-down the Cypriot understanding of coercion which, at present, could potentially include any form of relief and development work which included evangelism as well. Of course, there are understandable historical reasons why Cyprus might be sensitive about such issues and their case is emblematic of broader sensitivities in parts of Europe, such as the Balkans, particularly where there has been historic tension and strife between Christians and Muslims.

There is a vortex of often contrary issues being played out across the continent at present which the EU as an institution appears to be doing its best to keep out of. The Commission would dearly love religion to disappear quietly into the night as secularisation theorists have been predicting would happen for centuries. However, that hasn't happened and does not look likely to happen. So, as much as they try and keep religion out of the way either by passing the problems to member state level, or by spending more time focussing on external FoRB issues than internal ones, there is one specific area which the EU has had to engage with religion: Islamic radicalisation. Concerns over this have come about as a result of the bombings and arrests in numerous European cities, but has been forced to the surface by the acknowledgement that radicalisation is increasing, rather than decreasing, across the continent.

The EP has expressed particular concern about the teaching of some *madrassas* operating in different parts of the EU as being one source of radicalisation. On 15th November, 2012 the Swedish MEP Olle Schmidt reflected this concern when he led a panel discussion in the EP about the link between education and radicalisation.[21] Acknowledging the growth of radicalisation has also prompted the development of the EU's own counter terrorism (CONTEST) strategy.[22]

Concerns over radicalisation are keeping religion on the agenda internally. Some of that engagement has spilled over into broader 'inter-cultural dialogue' (the EU focus in 2008) which acknowledges that radicalisation is not born in a vacuum, and thus a certain level of engagement with broader issues of cohesion and integration is required. Yet this is difficult for the EU, for there is increasing pressure from nationalist parties across many member states who see any language of 'integration' as a Trojan Horse for increased EU fed-

---

[21] The report upon which that discussion is based is here http://europeandemocracy.eu/2012/11/radicalisation-in-schools-and-universities/ (1st April 2014).

[22] Information and documents concerning the EU's CONTEST work can be accessed through their website http://europa.eu/legislation_summaries/justice_freedom_security/fight_against_terrorism/l33275_en.htm (1st April 2014).

eralism. There is a real sense in which the EU as an organisation is unable to fully address cohesion issues, because they risk further alienating the kinds of nationalist parties that are making more rapid gains at member level and EP levels. For that reason, the EU CONTEST strategy has needed to be primarily intelligence-focussed to the detriment of creating an inclusive narrative which might counter the voices of disaffection which can be the basis for terrorist recruitment.

4. Summary

Encapsulating the broad sweep of trends that form the back-drop to chapters concerning evangelism to Muslims is a nearly impossible task. Hopefully, I have provided a sufficient sense of the backdrop within which the grass-roots work of mission to Muslims in Europe is taking place. More particularly, this chapter has hopefully given a sense of the EU's perspectives on engagement with religion generally, and FoRB especially, so that we can understand how questions of 'blasphemy' and 'proselytisation' are approached by those in authority over us.

As we continue the work of bringing Christ to those who do not yet know Him several matters are worth reiterating as a reference. Firstly, EU officials have inherited a deep sense of distrust about religion in a Europe born of a centuries-old conflict which has manifested in the 'EU era' as a desire to keep religion out of the public square without being seen to be shutting it out, until such time as it dies out of its own accord. Secondly, FoRB campaigning by Muslims particularly, as well as Christians and atheists, are creating mounting problems for the EU as it seeks to pass such issues off to national governments whilst loudly pronouncing on the ills of other FoRB abuses beyond its boarders. Thirdly, even if the FoRB campaigning was not occuring, concerns over radicalisation mean that religion has to be engaged with, at least for the moment, even though political constraints mean that it cannot offer an alternative vision to the radicalisers. Fourthly, despite a strong right-wing reaction to Muslim advocacy across the continent, the EU's need for money has opened it to the increased use of shari'a financial instruments. Fifthly, Islam has been the primary driver of religious consciousness in the EU over the last ten years as European Muslims adapt to a society (or series of societies) in which the critical examination of ideas, and the mocking of them if desired, is deemed acceptable, even beneficial and in which there is little sense that the state will intervene to protect religion.

CHAPTER 4

Engaging with Muslim Women in Europe
Elsie Maxwell

For a number of years I have been sharing my faith, my story, with many Muslim women. I have seen women accept the Gospel, but there are certain difficulties or areas which they find hard to understand. Some of the problems are my problems: Do I understand the women correctly? Do I understand their culture, their worldview, their learning style, their language, and their particular practices of the Islamic faith?

This chapter cannot cover the areas of the need to study and understand Islam for which there are many books and course which can help you do that. In this chapter, I will give some keys that I have found helpful in unlocking the Gospel for Muslim women.

My own heart and mind

First, I need to unlock my heart and my mind to them. This means I have already begun to know the Lord's passion for these women to hear about Christ. But now I am going to learn what it means to become their true friend. What is a true friend? Many people often say, 'I have a Muslim friend but I am afraid if I tell her about Christ she will no longer be my friend.' A true friendship means you both are able to share your love, accepting one another, enjoying many of lives' joys together and share your agreements and differences of life style and faith. One will want to learn and explore ways of sharing Christ which help people to want to listen to the message. It is helpful to view the situation as: "this is my life; my walk with Christ is to live my daily life as among Muslim women and others. It is my life, not ministry or job." Thus friends are not on my weekly schedule, but in my life 24/7; we can see each other any time or place. This becomes even much more important when they become believers.

Spending some time in language learning or at least learning some useful words and phrases is so helpful. Language learning also opens the door to understanding culture.

Understanding culture and worldview

It is very useful to understand culture and worldview – how they think and learn. A good way to start is to write out you own worldview first. List the important factor of a western worldview and comment on your own Christian views.

A western worldview

Family: Great emphasis is placed on the individual; the goal is to be self-reliant. Successful people make their own choices. The family is the couple and the children (two or three). Most couples share the care of the children and the home. Men are sometimes the full-time caregiver of the children. Extended family may live nearby or far away.

Education: Learning happens by logical reasoning and deduction. University education is accessible for all, and greatly valued for careers and jobs.

Religion: Everyone is free to choose or not to choose, or change, it is a personal matter. It is acceptable to be unreligious. Moral behaviour was previously based on Judeo-Christian ideas, but these values are no longer held by many people.

Health: Great stress is placed on fitness, nutrition, diets, medical discoveries, and many hospitals.

Politics: Democracy allows people to choose the leaders, and change them. Anyone can choose to participate in politics. People are elected to a law making body and they can make laws or change laws. The law is not fixed by religion. Most Western countries have a Judeo-Christian background and consider that the Ten Commandments gave a foundational base to their law system. Many no longer hold these values in the same regard.

Leisure: This is considered an essential part of life: vacations, travel, sports, handicrafts, cinema, theatre, and opera. Not everyone can participate equally in all these things as they are often costly.

After listing the Western worldview, think about the following questions before reflecting on the Muslim worldview.
- What is my worldview as a Christian?
- Where do I differ from these general ideas?

The muslim worldview

Family: The family is the focus of life, the single unit or whole group which is where things happen and are centred and not the individual. Some families still have a sort of patriarchal structure but, even those that do not, the roles of the elders and the fathers are greatly respected. The extended family may no longer live together, younger members will accept the decisions and opinions of elders. There is security and safety within this framework. The tradition of arranged marriages and the marrying of close relatives continues. Women's roles have changed, but they bear the major work of the home and child care.

Education: The learning style of most Muslims is rote learning and memorisation.

Living in Europe means their learning is most likely not in their mother tongue. The Arabic language adds a layer of complexity to the religious Qur'anic Arabic which is unlike the daily spoken language. For some, this religious Arabic is considered 'high' Arabic, better and purer than the spoken. Some would even despise the dialect.

Religion: You are born a Muslim. It is understood as who you are. To be a Moroccan is to be a Muslim. It is not a private choice. It is you, your family, your community and your nation. Religion encompasses all. It directs your life: sleeping eating, drinking, food and shopping, education, work, marriage, children and death.

Health: God wills whatever happens and most people easily accept God's will. Sometimes they seem to have a fatalistic view of life.

Politics: Strong leaders are respected. For many young people, democracy is not seen as a legitimate way for Muslims, as it is man-made with man-made laws. They would prefer the Shari'a law. But at the present, there is much political unrest.

Leisure: It is not a priority but nevertheless many enjoy sports and music. Muslim holidays are happy and busy socialising times for the family.

Here are two further questions to help you evaluate the Muslim worldview.
- What areas are important to me? Would my ideas clash with the Muslim worldview?
- What areas of the Muslim view are attractive to me?

Love

Love is the most important key to unlocking the heart and mind of our friends. This may seem overly simplistic, as you would say: 'Of course I love them.' But how is love expressed? What factors or actions enable it to be understood?

In most cultures, body language and gestures are as important as the words spoken. Eastern women like to be bodily close to the person to whom they are speaking, shaking their hands – embracing and kissing are very normal actions. The focus is very person-centred and not time-centred. We are not always conscious of how time-centred we are as Westerners. A friend of mine used to often knit while she visited, as she felt just sitting about talking was a time waster. It is often joked that Westerners have watches, but Easterners have time. One needs to be as unhindered by time commitments as is possible in a western world setting.Words and speech are used in more abundance and with more flourish than English. I found that asking them how to say various things was extremely helpful in learning how to use words. They feel honoured to help you and needed rather than always on the receiving end.[1]

---

[1] Joy Loewen, *Women to Women, Sharing Jesus with a Muslim Friend*. Baker Publishing Gp (2010).

Hospitality

Hospitality is given high priority in an honour/shame culture – a wonderful door, which gives opportunity to express and share love with them rather than to them.

Often they prefer that we come to their homes, where they feel safe and comfortable. We need to accept their offers and enjoy their homes, their food, their ways and their expressions of love to us. Learning to be truly comfortable with them can be an adventure: eating with your hands, eating some unusual foods, sleeping in a room with others, often surrounded by many people. For most of the people groups I have known, it is the custom to bring small gifts either for the mother or the children. Often gifts of homemade food are appropriate. It is not the cost but the gesture of giving. Their culture is extremely generous and ours may seem more selfish in comparison. I was often overwhelmed with gifts. After the visit, try to take a few minutes to evaluate what you learned from them and observed about the home life and living styles. From you reflections, you can plan what to do when they visit your home. Greetings at the door are really important. Each person is being received and accepted with all the special words and kisses. Remember the story of how Simon asked Jesus to his home but didn't welcome him properly.

Will your house have a natural feeling of welcome? Are there offensive pictures, objects or animals? Have you prepared acceptable food? Many Muslim women seem to have very low self-esteem, your acceptance of them, leads to trusting you and in turn, will open the door for them to listen to you speak about Christ. Spending unrushed time having coffee or tea with friends is extremely valuable way to build good friendships. Ask the Lord to help you to be more comfortable in others' homes and to relax and to enjoy all the differences, not be fearful and to learn to ask questions.

Effective communicating with oral learners

One thing I often notice is the confusion that sometimes exists between telling and teaching. Telling is not the same as teaching. Teaching has a specific plan, preparation for the person or people one will teach. At the appointed time, the teacher teaches it. The plan takes into consideration the learner's style of learning. In the Western cultures, we general take it for granted that everyone learns the same way. However, recently there has been a great deal of effort to consider the learner's learning style: Oral, Print/readers, or a combination of styles.[2] The oral learner will find it hard to grasp the knowledge if presented

---

[2] Roland Muller, *The Messenger, The Message, The Community* (along with Honor and Shame) are available to download: http://canbooks.com; R. Muller (penname) give rich insights on how oral learners perceive the Gospel.

in a style he does not easily understand. But we must not think of oral learners as illiterate; they may read books, but this is not their basic learning method. Knowledge is gathered in the group or community from one another. Knowledge is passed from person to person, listening to the story of how that person experienced or achieved something.

Some principles of oral learning[3]

1. The story or stories is one of the main formats of knowledge. It is often heard in a small group and not just one to one.

2. A story is a bigger concept than mere words or points. It does not happen in isolation but touches the whole picture of a person: her life, her actions, the results and relates some sort of message about what or why this happened. The story becomes the message. Various types of stories are told in everyday life: some are personal real-life stories, a parable, a proverb, a picture, in DVD format, drama or in musical form.

3. The Bible narratives so clearly fit the above pattern of learning. If you use a chronological format, giving the story a time frame means you are giving an oral Bible to the person. Those who become believers will have this knowledge for further spiritual growth.

4. The wonderful part is that stories are easily remembered and are often repeated to others, spreading the message in a very natural way.

5. These learners enjoy memorising and will readily memorise stories and Bible verses. You can freely teach memory verses as part of the story.

6. Stories are not passive. When hearing the story, the learners enter into it, feeling the emotions, relating to the experiences of those in the story. This style uses more of the senses and easily engages the listeners to respond. Asking questions plays a major role. (Use 'WH' words: why, where, when, who, how, what. ie: Who is God speaking to? What did he say? Did the person respond, 'Yes'? What happen then? What would you do?) The story enables them to enter into the situation without feeling threatened or embarrassed.

---

[3] More information on oral learning and orality can be obtained from the following articles/websites: Cameron D. Armstrong, "The Efficiency of Storying." Evangelical Missions Quaterly, Billy Graham Centre Wheaton (available online); July 2013, page 322ff – Phil Thornton, "Contextual Teaching: Changes in Content & Culture", "Evangelical Missions Quarterly" (available online); July 2013, page 342ff – The International Orality Network has many resources on their website: http://www.orality.net – John Piper, "Missions, Orality, and the Bible: thoughts on Pre-, Less- and Post-literate Cultures." http://www.desiringgod.org/articles/missions-orality-and-the-bible.

7. The message is being heard and seen in action, not just abstract facts. Good and bad actions are seen and difficult information is less confrontational in this format. The logical pattern of thinking is not linear from A to B to C, but rather seeing how things work, or do not work in real life issues in a person's life. Westerners often find this style more uncomfortable, as they were taught in a logical linear pattern.
8. Jesus used this teaching style in the daily life situations: need of food, in a storm, meeting the needs of a sick person.

If you want to explore a bit more about learning styles and which style is the style best matching your friend, you can download an orality assessment tool from the internet.[4]

Use Scripture

It is the work of the Holy Spirit to help people to understand truth and to convict of sin. Our role is to properly handling the Word of truth. That is why I wanted to speak about our communication skills first. You may also want to refresh your memory of Islam's main points of belief and the major objections your friend may have about Christianity. Then you will be better able to choose and prepare appropriate stories to share in this style.

1. Choose stories: from Creation to Christ (10-12)
2. Choose stories from Luke
3. Choose stories about women in the Bible
4. Choose stories of people who prayed and how God answer

You need to write down your personal story of how you came to Christ: explaining life before knowing Christ, the salvation experience and everyday life with Christ now. After you write your story, make sure it is fairly short and precise, that the words are not just Christian cliché words, and that your Muslim friends could easily understand their meanings.

Prayer

The other key which many converts mentioned is prayer. Your stories will bring up question and responses. I encourage them to respond to God Himself. After the creation story, you could just simply say thank you for the various things you enjoy of God's creation. This gives each one an opportunity to speak personally to God in their own words.

---

[4] http://fjseries.org/low/Orality_Assessment_Tool_Worksheet.pdf.

When people mention problems or needs you can also pray with them, speaking personally to God for them. But when the answers come, it is important to remember to thank God, acknowledging it is God who heard and answers prayer.

Of course prayer is ultimately a very important part of all we do: loving others, hospitality, sharing the stories, and praying with them. It is God's work and it is a wonderful privilege to be a part of His world plan.

Conclusion

Many times people ask if there is a special way or key to ministry among Muslim women. Unfortunately, the answer to this question is, 'No': there is not a special way or key. I believe it is a combination of factors which we learn through experience and our own spiritual maturity and growth in ministry. Learning to understand people, their culture, ways of life and learning, gave me the impetus to learn different styles of teaching, and fitting my teaching to the person's style of learning. If we are to pick out one factor to highlight above others, it would be LOVE. May we learn not only to love others but also to be able to express our love in manner they understand.

CHAPTER 5

Engaging with Muslims in Mosques[1]

Andreas Maurer

There are many different ways for Christians to encounter Muslims and share the truth about Jesus. In this chapter, I wish to focus on meeting Muslims at their local mosques. I am often confronted by Christians who think it is impossible to visit a mosque to make friends with Muslims and share the Gospel. Not all mosques are open for Christian visitors but, unless you ask, you will never know if a mosque is open for visits or hosts events open to non-Muslims. Let me point out a few basic guidelines which have been observed in successful encounters.

1. Guidelines for visiting people in a mosque

Preparation

The Christian layman or leader should make an appointment with the leader of the mosque to discuss the format of visits for both Christian men and women. It is advisable that a Christian woman is accompanied by a man, unless she has already established friendships with Muslim women from the mosque. After introductions, you should state the reasons why you want to visit. It may be a general interest in their religion and culture, or the desire to establish better relations between Muslims and Christians. You should affirm that you are there to listen and learn, but that you also wish to explain your understanding of spiritual truth.

Ask the leaders what weekly meetings you as a Christian may attend (whether for men or women). Ask if there are facilities open to the public, such as a library, where you can study their faith or meet Muslims willing to discuss certain topics. It is important that protocol is clarified to avoid unnecessary offense i.e. Christians should remove their shoes before entering; observe any particular mosque's rules, and all should dress conservatively. A helpful rule is "If you do not ask, you will not know." Remember: each mosque has a different set up, activities and schedule. However, there is no need to partake in ritual washing and recited prayer. By doing these things, Muslims may assume

---

[1] Please see also my book "Ask your Muslim friend", AcadSA Publishing, 2008, ISBN 978-1-920212-26-1, section 3.2.4, www.aymf.net.

that you want to join the Islamic religion. During their prayers you may sit in the back, quietly observe ... and pray for them!

Actual visitation

It is better to go in the name of an organisation, your local church or as an individual. Muslims can be wary of Christian missions, associating their activities with the Crusades or with attempts to gain converts by offering material help. If it is your first visit to a particular mosque, ask a guide for a tour. They may feel insulted if, as a Christian, you just walk in. Be sensitive and ask for permission to do things such as taking pictures. Never walk in front of Muslims praying. Always be friendly and polite. Partake in any refreshments if served afterward, be sure to chat with Muslims and express gratitude for their hospitality. Ask how long you may visit, and leave at the agreed time.

Listen carefully and show an interest in what is said. Earn the right to speak through mutual respect. Questions should only be asked on the topics the Muslims have spoken about. Do not 'preach' at them in the mosque (consider your reaction if the roles were reversed). You may be more direct at a personal meeting with them later at their home. Once you have established friendships, you may visit the mosque on a regular basis on your own.

During any discussions, the Christian group should always follow their leader's instructions and example. Never ask aggressive or insulting questions.[2] At times you may politely ask for Quranic references on statements they make (say that you have a Quran at home and would like to look it up yourself). If they cannot answer your questions, do not press the matter. You may give the biblical view at the appropriate time, but keep your responses short and to the point.

Christians may also invite the Muslims to visit their church e.g. to explain to them the facilities and to give a talk on the message of the Bible. This should be done out of a desire to return hospitality.

2. Speaking with ordinary Muslims in a mosque

Muslims are normal human beings: rather liberal and mainly interested in living a quiet and happy life. They have desires, hopes, joys and pain like everyone else. It is not for a Christian to teach Muslims about their faith, but rather to ask relevant questions to make them think about their faith in the Creator.

Though Muslims are interwoven in their community, we should avoid stereotyping and view each of them as a unique individual. Show a keen interest in them and listen carefully to what they have to say. Like Christians, they do not all believe in the same way. Ask them about their individual life and religious practice.

---

[2] Ibid., I present sample questions at the end of the chapters.

It is important to understand their inner tensions: though outwardly they appear confident, in their hearts they often have doubts as to what true Islam really is. Additionally, the value systems of a liberal modern democracy are in stark contrast to the conservative Islamic theocracy of the Quran. Recognize the cultural differences. Young Muslims are torn between their 'home' western culture and their parents' origins, particularly concerning issues about women.

Engaging with Muslims is a challenge but not a threat to Christians, for Jesus said: "All authority in heaven and on earth has been given to Me ... surely, I will be with you always, to the very end of the age" (Mt. 28:18-20). Take the initiative to start a conversation. Initially, talk about general, everyday topics. Listen first; then talk into their situation. Pay attention to their worries and fear. You may also offer to pray for them. If you pray in their presence, address God as the Creator.

Christians are encouraged to explain their faith naturally to Muslims. Explain how you came to faith in Jesus and how you practically experience your daily walk with God. Use words which Muslims can understand. If they mention Islamic religious issues, ask for a reference. If the situation arises, be prepared to read the Quran or other Islamic literature with them. This should, in fairness, allow you to read Bible references and relevant Christian literature on the same topic. Offer to spend time with them explaining the teaching of the Bible, always emphasizing the uniqueness of Jesus Christ.[3]

Should a Christian use the Quran in discussions? If a Muslim does not say anything about Islam, Muhammad or the Quran, then I as a Christian will also not do so. When, however, a Muslim refers to the Quran, I am happy to read and discuss its topics. However, my aim is to go to the Bible as soon as possible, asking my Muslim friend: Would you mind if we read about this topic in the Bible? Indeed, Christians should have good knowledge about the Quran, but their knowledge of the Bible should be far greater.

Meeting Muslims in a mosque is, in many ways, no different than meeting them elsewhere. However, those who 'go to mosque' are largely devoted in their faith and actually more approachable in discussing religious issues. If allowed, I also distribute tracts and other Christian literature, including the Bible, in mosques. I ask them to read it and, if they have any questions, they can ask me. Depending on their questions, I will use the appropriate Bible passages to answer their questions. If, for instance, we speak about Abraham or another prophet, I will use the relevant Bible references in the Old and New Testament. In addition, I may give them a separate sheet where the relevant

---

[3] These guidelines are outlined in my book "Ask your Muslim Friend", section 3.2.1.

references to this topic are written.[4] My experience is that Muslims have higher respect for Christians who explain and stand for the whole truth of the Bible!

I have found it good to visit three mosques in rotation – one mosque per month. It is not wise to visit too frequently, as this may make Muslims uncomfortable. Sometimes I go to simply listen and learn, only speaking if asked. Be wise in how you use words and literature, always acting in such a way that a door is left open for further visits. Never hide tracts throughout a mosque for Muslims to discover later; such actions only cause bad feelings and may close the door. Christians should be open and honest in word and deed. If a Christian is unprepared to take off shoes or observe regulations, or otherwise feels uncomfortable, he or she should not visit a mosque. There are many other places to naturally meet Muslims in your community.

3. Discussions with Muslim leaders and scholars

The same guidelines apply to discussions with Muslim leaders. Always meet the leader of the mosque before an initial visit to discuss details. It is never necessary to act or compromise out of fear. Christians should be sufficiently confident to approach Muslim leaders with respect and an open mind. If you explain the truth in a loving way, Muslims respect you more than if you avoid or fail to explain your faith in Jesus Christ.

When Muslim leaders explain Islam, politely ask for the references. Be ready to study the Quran with them and then point to the Bible, reading the relevant passage together. When I visit a mosque, I like to give a Bible to the leader as a present. As a holy book, it should not be full of pictures or colour.

I was once invited by a Muslim scholar to his home. He offered me to present my faith for thirty minutes, challenging me to show the important points of my faith and their implications. He then intended to present his faith, also within half an hour, eager to prove that Islam is superior to every other religion, including Christianity. I focused on presenting the Christian faith as it develops from the Old Testament with its sacrificial system, and concluded by emphasizing its climax in the New Testament: Jesus dying at the cross as the final and perfect sacrifice. By explaining the Gospel, I emphasized the most important two points: firstly, that by believing in Jesus Christ, God gives me eternal life as a gift and, secondly, God guarantees me that, after death, I will enter paradise (heaven).

The Muslim scholar seemed impressed by my faith and conviction, saying that, if this is truly my faith, then Islam has nothing higher to offer. He was even

---

[4] Ibid., section 3.4.1.

reluctant to use his half-hour! This experience encouraged me, whenever possible, to explain boldly my faith in Jesus, who says that He is the truth (Jn. 14:6).

In another mosque, the leader informed me that there was a Quran study group on Thursday evenings which I, as a Christian, could attend. First, a passage in the Quran was read and the group discussed the text, trying to understand its meaning. Often the interpretation and understanding varied widely amongst group members. The leader then asked me to explain what the Bible has to say on the particular topic – a wonderful opportunity to explain the message of the Bible to this group of Muslims in the mosque. Not in every mosque offers such possibilities but, unless you ask, you will never know what possibilities there are.

On another occasion, I was allowed to visit a mosque library to sit and read. Some Muslims approached me and we had interesting talks about faith issues. They asked about comparative themes in the Bible. One man gave me his card and mentioned that he wanted to meet me outside the mosque. He had questions about the Christian faith, but did not want his other friends to know of his interest in the message of the Bible.

During mosque visits, I like to meet Muslim friends and ask about their life and faith in the Creator. I trust God for the right appointments. I am open to meet any Muslim willing to talk. I can participate in group discussions but I prefer to talk with individuals, as people in groups do not share with open hearts. Often a Muslim invites me to his private home at a later date where we can discuss issues about faith privately. If there is a need, I offer to pray for their particular requests. This prayer can be done in a silent corner of the mosque or anywhere else later. It is important, however, that my friend agrees to it. I make sure as I pray that my friend can understand my terminology. In addition to praying for a friend in his presence, I also pray for him in my own personal prayer time.

I also visit mosques if there are special feasts or gatherings e.g. breaking the fast of Ramadan *(Eid)*, and the sacrifice in remembrance to Abraham *(Eid-ul-Adha)*. However, I will only go if I have a personal invitation from a Muslim taking part. It is important to be informed about the implications involved. For instance, if they present meat or other food which has been offered in a sacred Islamic way, I must decide if I will eat it or not and my explanation for doing so. It is vital to not give the impression that I am on my way to becoming a Muslim. Whatever we do or say, we can send such 'signals'. Of course, Muslims have challenged me many times: why do I come to the mosque? Do I intend to convert them? I make it clear that I cannot convert any person; rather, it is a matter between a person and Almighty God. Only God can change the heart of a person.

Occasionally, I tell stories such as this:

Imagine a young man, age 20, who has learned that there are many different religions in the world. He notices that there are similarities, but also contradictions. He decides to go into all the world to study all religions in order to find the truth. After 30 years of travelling and studying, he returns to his home village, overjoyed because he found the only true God and the truth about Him. He feels secure knowing that, after death, he will be in paradise. He says to himself: "What a lucky man I am! I know the true God and the truth about Him. I can now enjoy the rest of my life and relax. Why should I bother about my parents, my relatives and friends who do not know God and the truth about Him? Though they will surely go to hell, the main thing is that I know the truth and how to enter paradise." I then ask my Muslim friend what he thinks about this man who found the truth but does not share it with his people of the village. The answer will be: "This is truly a selfish man; he should share his knowledge and experience with other people so that they too, can accept the truth." I then explain to my Muslim friend that this is exactly what I am doing. I am convinced that God showed me the truth and I want them also to know it. However, I make it clear that I am also interested in listening to what they understand the truth to be.

4. Introducing and organizing special 'MFBU' meetings[5]

Of the many possible ways of having peaceful meetings between people of different faiths, I offer the 'Meeting For Better Understanding' (MFBU). The purpose is not to hold debates or criticize each other, nor to create a unified religion, but to facilitate the presentation of various faiths by their proponents so that misunderstandings and misconceptions may be exposed and a better understanding of others' faith be reached. The goal is to foster new friendships of mutual respect.

Muslims and Christians in a community agree to meet together, alternatively in the mosque and the church. Preparatory meetings will review arrangements and guidelines in detail which are agreed to by an organizing committee consisting of equal numbers of Christians and Muslims.

One representative of each religion has 30 minutes to present a talk on an agreed topic. After the two presentations, a further session of 30 minutes is allotted to questions and answers. An appointed moderator, accepted by both parties, will direct this session. Only questions directed to the topic will be allowed. People should refrain from aggressive or insulting questions or remarks. Both sides may present relevant literature (free or for sale) which informs those attending about the teaching of both faiths.

---

[5] Ibid., section 3.5.5.

A more relaxed time of meeting each other should follow at a place where individual conversations and discussions may take place and light refreshments are served.

If some participants, as a result, change their religion, will each faith community tolerate such behaviour? This issue, though delicate and inflammatory, must be addressed openly. If one faith community has a problem with such freedom of religion, the matter needs to be clarified and an agreement reached. The Christian perspective is that Christians cannot convert Muslims; rather, conversion is the work of the Spirit of God.

The topics of MFBU events may be religious, social or a blend thereof. Some suggested topics are:

Religious	Social
1) The unity of God	1) Human rights and religious freedom
2) What is 'sin'? How does man enter paradise?	2) Morality and honesty
3) Who is Jesus Christ? Who is Muhammad?	3) Family life: Husband – wife – children relationships
4) Bible and Quran: origin and inspiration	4) Marriage
5) Relationship of man to God	5) Upbringing of children in your local society
6) What are the marks of a true prophet?	6) Basic rules of friendship and neighbourhood
7) The attributes of God/Allah	7) What is the cause of terror?
8) Prayer and fasting	8) How could war be avoided?
9) What are the marks of a true Christian/Muslim?	9) Why is there so much corruption?
10) Definition of the Church/Umma	10) Cultural life
11) What happens on the day of judgment?	11) How can a peaceful life between different races be achieved?

To conduct such MFBU events demands great effort and courage. Both communities, Christians and Muslims, need to be positive about such meetings, but it is worth investing in such endeavours. As Christians and Muslims talk with each other and learn more about the other's faith, they learn to respect and appreciate each other. They also learn more about life in the church and the mosque. Personal friendships will develop that allow people to meet privately.

5. Various possible meetings in the mosque

In the above chapters I have outlined ways to meet Muslims in their mosques and hopefully build bridges of friendships with some of them. As Christians, we can visit Muslims during their prayer times in the mosque and, as trust builds, engage in friendly conversation. We can visit them at their various facilities within the mosque: reading in the library and having discussions; drinking and eating together at the mosque cafeteria; or meet the man who sells Islamic items at the mosque shop. Organizing alternative talk evenings (MFBU), which focus on agreed topics at each event, can involve the whole community. Most other meetings are in smaller groups or just on a one to one basis. It is my experience, that the most beneficial conversations are held on a private location, where individual discussions are possible. Of course, meeting Muslims is possible not only in the mosque but at other places as well, public or private. The best kinds of encounters, whether in mosques, churches or elsewhere, are socially natural.

CHAPTER 6

Engaging with Muslim Youth

Anne-Käthi Degen

Fatima grew up in Switzerland with a Catholic mother and a Muslim father from the Middle East. She is a dedicated 19-year-old Muslim girl, wears tight jeans and the veil by conviction. Her apprenticeship goes well and she has started to earn money. Whilst she is actively engaged in the youth group of the local mosque, she also attends events organised by Muslim youth organisations throughout the country. On the other hand, there is a 16-year-old Turkish Muslim girl, who goes clubbing every weekend. Alcohol seems to be only *haram* at home and she has had sexual relations before marriage. Living a double life is exhausting.

And what about Blerim? When he was ten years old, he had to leave his home country Macedonia. His father had already been working as a seasonal worker abroad and was finally able to bring along his family. Now, his parents live from welfare. Blerim had many difficulties in school; his marks and his behaviour left a lot to be desired. His friends consider him as religious, although he seldom goes to the mosque nor performs his prayers regularly. But talking to him one feels that his faith is important. He loves to talk about religious matters and often adds superstitious elements.

The range of young Muslim identities could be expanded with many more examples including converts, homosexuals etc. This chapter of the book deals with one specific youth culture (the *Islamic Youth Culture*), one model of engagement (dialogue with young people in the UK) and practical and theological considerations for youth work among Muslims and Christians.

The reason for engaging with Muslim youth lies first of all in a passion and joy to encounter young Muslims. There is the need to build a society in which Christian, Muslim and other faith groups are able to cooperate and live together peacefully. Muslim youth are going to be a factor in Europe's economic, political and social future. There is undoubtedly a call for integrating, training and equipping young people from all sorts of backgrounds to become mature people who take responsibility for the world they live in. I believe that Christians have a duty to be a true and trustworthy loving neighbour in practising the Christian faith among those people living around us. Being a loving neighbour and a counterpart implies giving answers and information about the Christian faith as well as in other areas of life, to challenge, to comfort, to discuss, to negotiate values, to pray, to be friends, to support. Young people are in a phase of shaping their opinions, of learning about other ways of life, of discovering life stories and reflecting on their own roots and history. In this phase, Christians can emerge as true counterparts and companions whose faith determines their way of life and gives witness to Christ.

Young people from a Muslim background are often the second or third generation to live in a Western country with German, English or French as their preferred language. Nevertheless, they often have strong connections to the country of their parents or relatives such as Pakistan, Kosovo or Turkey, which become their place for summer holidays. For some young Muslims their faith is important; others distance themselves from their roots as they immerse themselves into secular society. Some rediscover Islam in their late teenage years and deal intensively with matters of faiths by reading religious literature, watching 'YouTube preachers' or attending Islamic lectures. For this chapter, young Muslims are between 13 and 30 years old. Older ones often take a crucial lead with regards to youth work and above all in the *Islamic Youth Culture* – a religious youth culture of young Muslims.

Islamic Youth Culture

Whether we call it Pop-Islam or *Islamic Youth Culture*[1] it includes different motivations and emphases. Still, it can be described as combining Islam with Western culture, regaining a new identity as religious, 'cool' young Muslims in Europe. Music, fashion, blogs and magazines not only give this culture a face but most of all a voice to young religious Muslims. It is worth searching online for the music and the text of German Rapper *Ammar 114*, the music group *Poetric Pilgrimage* or listening to *Nasheeds*[2] (Islamic worship songs) strikingly similar to many Christian songs. The website www.muslimhiphop.com presents Muslim musicians from all over the world. One can browse T-shirts and accessories of *styleislam*. Islam is expressed on shirts, pointing to the *Ummah*, Mohammed or the *Shahada* (three fingers). Mohammed Ali, a graffitti painter from the UK, is known all over the globe and Internet platforms like *waymo*, the magazine *cube mag* or *Rivival* give insights to the heart and minds of young Muslims. The blog of the young Muslim woman Kübra Gümüsay[3] is a powerful voice of a multiple identity that is not only Muslim but also that of a young woman, traveller and journalist. At concerts, conferences, poetry slams

---

[1] See Gerlach, Julia; *Zwischen Pop und Dschihad* (Berlin: Ch. Links, 2006).

[2] *Lyrics Nasheed* "How can you deny", http://english.islammessage.com/article details.aspx?articleId=728 (31st January 2014).

[3] Kübra Gümüsay, *ein fremdwörterbuch*. http://ein-fremdwoerterbuch.com (31st January 2014) For English Blogs look at: http://ein-fremdwoerterbuch.com/cate gory/englishwords.

and other youth events women and men are equally present, although at some youth events gender segregation is taking place. The overall outcome is modern, self-confident and matches Western culture with Islam, while values point to an orthodox reading of the Qur'an. Nevertheless, theological opinions about how to live a Muslim life in Europe seem to be constantly discussed when certain stars as described above overstep boundaries (for example by wearing make up or dancing as a Muslim).

Islamic Youth Culture does not only promote the fusion of Islam and the West, it also helps young Muslims to find a new identity in Islam and become more confident. British young Muslims often show a more positive perception of society as they acknowledge the freedom and tolerance of their activities within their country. German and French Muslims feel less accepted.[4] Some young Muslims strive to counter the misconception of Islam as they have suffered from negative news reports about Islam since the events of 9/11. They want to represent Islam positively and tell society that they are normal people who can contribute to society in a positive way. Some have a message that might arise from their beliefs but which can still be addressed to everyone, such as the calling for peace. Others, however, use this subculture as a means to make *Da'wah* (inviting people to embrace Islam) among people both with a Muslim background and non-Muslims.

The majority of young people from a Muslim background are rarely involved in this culture. Nevertheless, this scene has been growing in the last 10 years and has professionalised its websites and performance. The strong Internet presence and self-confident young Muslims have an impact on other young Muslims.

Poetic Pilgrimage
Source:
www.muslimhiphop.com.

---

[4] See Herding, M., Inventing the Muslim Cool, Islamic Youth Culture in Western Europe (Bielfeld: transcript, 2013).

One cover of the *revival*, a magazine for young Muslims in Britain.
Source: www.therevival.co.uk.

Source: www.styleislam.com.

Models of engagement – Dialogue

Looking at the specific *Islamic youth culture,* but also at the wide range of other young Muslims, raises the question of how Christians can engage with them. Young Muslims are diverse. While religious young Muslims might be more interested in learning about the Christian faith and getting to know practising Christians (they realise that not every Westerner can be equated with Christians), other young Muslims search for a place to be at home, to find friends and have fun. This chapter will not map out one model suitable for every Christian and Christian group that aims to engage with young Muslims. While some Christians offer to help with homework or job searching, others have invited young Muslims to participate in sports group or youth groups. Some of these activities and programmes convey a 'Christian message', either evangelistic or carrying values that challenge or support both Christians and Muslims. This chapter looks specifically at the model of dialogue, which is obviously not the sole model of engagement. Dialogue best suits those Christian and Muslim youths who have dealt with faith issues and come with a base of faith knowledge and experience. Young Christians who are rooted within their faith will easily find connections with young religious Muslims as they discover they have many religious convictions and values in common. One does not need to start by discussing the existence of God or the day of judgement. Further exchange will bring forth more commonalities and differences. Both sides will be challenged not only to revise their preconceptions but also to think through theological matters and each one's foundation. What makes each religion distinct? Who is Christ for Christians? Such questions probe the very foundations of how faith and religion are understood. Religious young Muslims are often trained to give answers about their faith. Islamophobia has caused the need for information, the need to explain themselves and Islam. Young Christians, on the other hand, often have to relearn to articulate their belief. Dialogue is a good exercise. In the light of the Islamic faith of these young religious Muslims, young Christians are forced to find a language to communicate faith matters. This does not only include apologetic answers; more often it asks for a lifestyle according to their Christian faith that is trustworthy and that gives witness to a faith that is often difficult to understand for Muslims: Why should Christians strive for a godly life if their sins are forgiven anyway?

Here is an example of a youth dialogue from an organisation based in the UK called *The Feast:*

The Feast – a model of a youth encounter by Andrew Smith

Scene: small groups making Venn diagrams of similarities and differences between Islam and Christianity.

Muslim girl: "What does this mean, 'Lamb of God'?"

Christian girl: "It's like a name for Jesus. Are there other names for God in Islam?"

Muslim girl: "Well, Islam has 99 names for God."

Christian girl: "Do you know any of them?"

Muslim girl: "I know some of them in English: God is the all-loving, the all-knowing, the most merciful, the compassionate, he's everywhere, he's all-forgiving…"

Christian girl: "Yeah, Christians believe all those things about God too! **Before I came on this weekend I would have thought we had nothing in common, but now I can see there's loads …**"

How many of us would love to have a conversation like that with our Muslim friends? How many of us would expect to hear that conversation between two teenage girls? Both these girls are passionate about their faiths but had formed such a close bond that they could engage in a discussion, albeit brief, that opened their eyes to a new understanding of the beliefs of the other person.

Conversations like that rarely happen just by chance and this one came as part of a structured program run by a UK based charity called The Feast (you can read more about this event and others at www.thefeast.org.uk). The work of The Feast came about through a desire to help Christian teenagers share their faith in a meaningful way with Muslims of their own age. The work tries to help young Christians take seriously, and be obedient to, the commandments that Jesus said were the most important: Love God and love you neighbour as yourself. This means being willing to listen as well as speak and seeking to build genuine friendships that aren't based on whether someone converts or 'responds to the Gospel'.

This model of work draws on good youth work practice and good interfaith dialogue work, combining them to create a space where young people meet, have fun and discuss topics relevant to them. The events are always small in number, typically five Muslims and five Christians as it's been found that a smaller number has a bigger impact on those involved. There is always a great emphasis put on trying to ensure equality of numbers so that there isn't, for example eight Christians and just two Muslims who could easily feel intimidated. There are always Christian and Muslim leaders, but as there are few young people the numbers needed are small. The groups tend to be one off events, but the young people are encouraged to come to a number of them.

At an event effort is put into breaking down fears or worries the young people might have through lively ice breaker games, this is followed by a faith discussion that almost always starts with the following question, 'What's the best thing about being a Christian or a Muslim?' Using this means the conversations flows in a positive way that allows people to share as much or little as they want. The discussion that follows adheres to some key principles. Firstly it's on a topic of interest to young people, so it's rarely abstract theology but relates to real life: eg the environment, home life, school etc. Secondly the young people are encouraged to share what they understand their faith teaches about that topic. This is a deliberate policy of equipping the young people to share their faith as they understand and experience it and not to try and quote leaders or scholars or to feel that they have to know everything. Thirdly the work presumes that the faith story the young people have is valid on its own terms and so is worth sharing and worthy of being listened to. Fourthly the work draws out both the similarities and differences between the faiths and encourages the young people to find ways to discuss difference peacefully. As a result of any event the young people are encouraged to think about how this is going to impact their life and the lives of others as they share the stories of what they did with friends and family members.

By being willing to meet, listen and to share their faith positively the young people often talk deeply about their faith and listen intently to the experiences and beliefs of others. Whilst it can be a very positive experience for the young people it, understandably, raises questions of whether this is an evangelistic endeavour or just for understanding or if dialogue exists for its' own sake. Many of the young people who come are passionate about their faith and would love to see others embracing the faith that they find reassurance and hope in (whether that's Islam or Christianity). The events do not lead to a point of inviting others to convert but do enable the young people to share their faith openly and in a way which doesn't demean or insult the beliefs of others. From a Christian perspective the work is based, partly on the exhortation in 1Timothy 3:15 to 'Always be prepared to give an answer to everyone who asks you to give the reason for the hope that you have. But do this with gentleness and respect,' (NIV). Some people are concerned that interfaith work is confusing for young people. When different beliefs are spoken of positively it can cause some to question what they believe and why. The anecdotal evidence is that the engagement, whilst raising questions, almost always encourages the young people to go and find out more about their own faith. Some youth leaders have talked about this as being a key method of discipleship as it's helping their young people to go much deeper in their own faith. The programmes are also set up so that the young people come with a leader so that they can discuss issues from the day afterwards allowing them to continue to process what they have experienced. This raises the question of what dialogue with young people can achieve. If run well it can lead to genuine friendships being made and serious, deep conversations about matters of faith. This leads to understanding and an ability to discuss difference in peaceful and constructive ways. Whilst it stops short of inviting people to convert it might lead to further conversations or invitations to other events at churches or mosques.

Theological considerations coming from youth dialogue

Genuine dialogue among religious young Christians and Muslims involves the sharing of things they are most passionate about, which often includes the sharing of faith. Witness is part of genuine dialogue and some young people might enter into dialogue with the desire for others to convert to Islam or to Christianity. Thus, a major concern people have about dialogue is whether people have a hidden agenda: Is dialogue just evangelism in disguise? There is a real danger that it can be, or that the work is merely a means to an end. Likewise, Muslims and others are suspicious whether friendships are being made or acts of service undertaken as a means to see people follow Christ. If Christians want to be trustworthy counterparts and companions, dealing with this issue is important. Then trust can be built between dialogue partners and friends.

In the past, there used to be a big divide between evangelistic and dialogue movements. Evangelism includes the proclamation of the Gospel that implies a call to a new life in Christ. Dialogue does not aim at inviting each other to convert. The two were considered to be incompatible with each other. In recent years, this view has been challenged by those who that good evangelism involves a relationship with those one is seeking to evangelise, which inevitably includes discussion and listening rather than simply preaching. On the other hand confessional dialogue[5] includes witness. One does not have to deny the desire to share the truths of one's own faith and to help others see its truth, joy and hope.

Nonetheless, there is a tension between evangelism and dialogue. This dilemma also holds true for Muslims who might want to engage in *Da'wah* whilst also being involved in a dialogue programme.

It is important how dialogue partners deal with this tension, even more so when dialogue is practised with young people. Being truthful relies on the importance of having no hidden agenda, of integrity and of informing about motivations and goals. Holding this tension requires a level of honesty and constant self-critique to make sure one is behaving with consistency. If dialogue is practised with young adolescents, it can be helpful to have an open discussion together with Christians and Muslims about motivations within dialogue.

Practical matters

Whether engaging with Muslim youth in a dialogue, at the church door, in a youth club or as neighbours the following points shall draw attention to some practical considerations:

Good youth work:

- Good youth work is relational. Spending time with young people and building relationships is the key for a flourishing youth work. Living in the area of participants of youth programmes is not always possible, but adds to a relationship that goes beyond the programme.

---

[5] See Cornille, C., *The Im-Possibility of Interreligious Dialogue* (New York: Herder & Herder Book, 2008).

- Good youth work tries to involve young people in the programme (participation). As helpers, actors in a drama/sketch, volunteers to set up the place, being interviewed on the stage or maintaining an online presence for the group, young Muslims (and Christians) are valued. Being part of the programme also means being part of the group. Delegating tasks and responsibilities will draw young people away from being consumers and eventually critiquing the programme to becoming supporters and co-leaders. They will enrich the programme with new ideas and projects.

- Good youth work contains fun elements and activities like sports, arts, nature activities as well as helping young people to grow spiritually and ethically. The activities might need to be slightly adapted: sports activities are better offered only for girls or boys and for overnight weekends it is mostly more difficult to get consent from parents, albeit not impossible.

Spiritual matters:

- Christian youth leaders and participants in a Christian youth group do not have to be afraid of talking about the Christian faith when young Muslims participate. The following has to be considered: young Muslims come with their own faith experience and religious convictions. Values like respect for elderly people, living a God-fearing life, doing good deeds can often be shared and discussed with young Muslims. The first commandment – love God and your neighbour – is considered to be common ground. Whilst there are terms and phrases that are common, e.g. forgiveness or grace, the understanding of the meaning of those can be very different and they therefore might need to be explained carefully.

- Young people should be allowed to say "no" to religious acts like prayers or singing religious songs if they do not agree with the content. The space to listen and observe without any pressure to practise the Christian faith is important. But it is appropriate to ask Muslims to show respect while others practise their faith.

- When Christian faith is preached, this implies that the Christian identity of the programme and the transparency about what is being done is evident for the young Muslim visitor and their parents. Young Muslims do not have to participate in the programme. The activity takes place in their free time. Parents can give consent when they know about the content of events. They also have the full right to decline and find a programme with religious or Christian content. Information about

Christian content and the organisation running the event should be noted on any publicity.

- What if a Muslim takes an interest in the Christian faith as a result of a church based youth programme? A teenager can learn about the Christian faith and discover Christ without changing his religion. Conversion will need to be handled carefully, as it is very likely to be difficult for the family to understand or support. Child protection rules will apply and the parents will need to be included in the decision even if they disapprove. Careful consideration will need to be given to how the person can be supported in their discipleship for many months or years to come. Perhaps, for some young Muslims seeking to follow Christ, the best advice is to go home and 'honour your father and mother'. Encouraging them to live out their faith in the home will, hopefully, provoke their parents to ask questions as they see the life-changing nature of an encounter with Jesus Christ. In a dialogue programme, it is possible that young people from either faith will start to find the faith of the others attractive. This is a challenge of any dialogue which we need to be aware of.

Other issues:

- If food is offered at a church youth event – which is always a good idea with young people – pork should be avoided and *halal* meat will need to be available for the Muslims. If young Christians and Muslims are together in dialogue, however, it is important to take into account different preferences for food for Christians as well as Muslims. They both have to learn to live with each other.

- Muslims have different opinions on music. More conservative Muslims would not approve of music and concerts, above all if they do not have religious content. For others, background music or concerts, singing in a choir or playing in a band is not a problem at all and can therefore be a common activity. Learning about their home and their religious habits will soon reveal the kind of Islam being practised.

- Some young Muslims are not used to being asked their opinion. They feel honoured to explain about their culture and religion in front of other participants. Nonetheless, Christian leaders have to pay attention not to take a Muslim teenager as a source of knowledge about a culture or Islam as the young boy or girl might not feel at ease due to minimal knowledge about his or her religious roots.

These practical ideas are given to help to think about how to do youthwork with Muslim young people in an ethical way. In whatever ways we engage with young Muslims, we will hopefully learn to love God and our neighbour. This first commandment also points to the Golden Rule, "So in everything do to others what you would have them do to you, for this sums up the Law and the Prophets." I often ask myself, "How do I want to become friends with others? how do I want to be served? In what way can I accept to be evangelised?" It will not necessarily solve all tensions but at least it will enhance an ethical encounter – with young Muslims.

CHAPTER 7

Engaging with Asylum Seekers
Paul Sydnor

When Jamal heard that I had come to visit, read the scriptures and pray with the asylum seekers passing through, he invited me into the wooden shelter. He was staying there temporarily until he could find transport to the next country. I took off my muddy shoes and stepped onto the floor, covered with blankets. It was a small wooden room, where fifteen asylum seekers crammed in to sleep each night. Eight of us gathered around in a circle on the floor. Jamal immediately showed a picture on his mobile of himself, dressed in white.

"This is me at Mecca. I went there over a year ago to find God, and I couldn't find him. Later, I explained this to 3 colleagues at work, and one of them said, 'If you want to find God, come to my home.' I went there and I met Jesus."

Soon after this, Jamal fled his country and crossed the sea to Europe. He then showed me another photo of himself dressed in white again, but this time for his baptism. He was baptised while on route to Europe as an asylum seeker. Now, some months later and several countries further, we sat together in a makeshift hut to discuss Jesus' own story of crossing the Sea of Galilee. Jamal's journey as an asylum seeker has taken him from place to place, fueled in the homes and visits of believers through hospitality.

Asylum Seekers in Europe

The top four countries of origin for Muslim immigrants from outside the EU are Algeria, Morocco, Turkey and Pakistan.[1] As the percentages show below, roughly a third of the immigrants in the EU are Muslim. In addition, Europe regularly receives over 300.000 new asylum seekers each year. In 2013, Syria, Russia, Afghanistan, Serbia, Pakistan, Kosovo, Somalia, Eritrea, Iran and Nigeria were the top ten origins of asylum seekers. At least half these are decidedly Muslim countries.[2]

---

[1] "Faith on the Move: The Religious Affiliation of International Migrants." 2012 ed. Washington D.C.: Pew Research Center's Forum on Religion and Public Life, 55.
[2] Statistics related to current asylum applicants in the EU is classified under "population", "migration and asylum" on the Eurostat webpage of the Europa website. http://epp.eurostat.ec.europa.eu/portal/page/portal/population/introduction.

Religious Composition of Immigrants in the European Union

Percentage and estimated number of **all immigrants** in the European Union by religious group

Percentage and estimated number of immigrants in the European Union (**excluding migration within the European Union**) by religious group

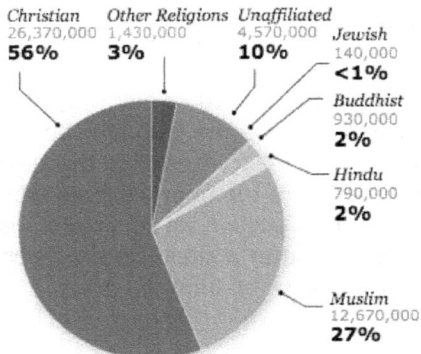

Christian 26,370,000 **56%**
Other Religions 1,430,000 **3%**
Unaffiliated 4,570,000 **10%**
Jewish 140,000 **<1%**
Buddhist 930,000 **2%**
Hindu 790,000 **2%**
Muslim 12,670,000 **27%**

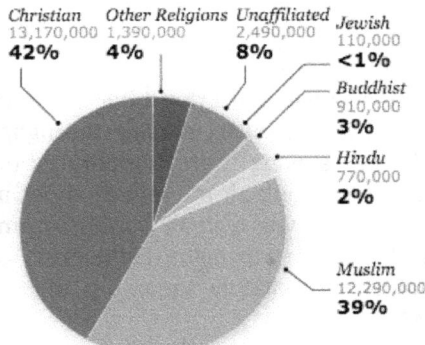

Christian 13,170,000 **42%**
Other Religions 1,390,000 **4%**
Unaffiliated 2,490,000 **8%**
Jewish 110,000 **<1%**
Buddhist 910,000 **3%**
Hindu 770,000 **2%**
Muslim 12,290,000 **39%**

Population estimates are rounded to ten thousands. Percentages are calculated from unrounded numbers and may not add to 100 due to rounding.

The 27 European Union countries are: Austria, Belgium, Bulgaria, Cyprus, Czech Republic, Denmark, Estonia, Finland, France, Germany, Greece, Hungary, Ireland, Italy, Latvia, Lithuania, Luxembourg, Malta, Netherlands, Poland, Portugal, Romania, Slovakia, Slovenia, Spain, Sweden and the United Kingdom.

Pew Research Center's Forum on Religion & Public Life • Global Religion and Migration Database 2010

Asylum seekers in the EU differ from refugees, in that they do not have an internationally recognized status, nor have they been accepted for immigration. They are in the process of becoming immigrants, and this can last from a few months to several years or more. This is often a difficult process because many asylum seekers do not fit the accepted and official categories for non-EU citizens such as guest laborers, skilled workers, family members or students. Their lives are vulnerable and their future is uncertain.

From the perspective of asylum seekers, social, political and economic conditions have uprooted and compelled them to leave their countries; this reality goes hand in hand with their cultural and religious identity. Nearly half of the asylum seekers in Europe are Muslim, so religion becomes the key category for understanding the shifting world order. These distinctions can lead to a conflict of religion with the threat of radical Islam on one end and the force of conservative Christians such as pentecostal and fundamentalism on the other. In order to break this cycle of socio-economic and religious tension, the church

---

See p. 7 of the report, "Asylum applicants and first instance decisions on asylum applications: 2013" for the 30 main citizenships of asylum seekers in 2013.

needs to understand the circumstances surrounding the asylum seekers among us, and reclaim the tradition of hospitality that both visits and welcomes the uprooted and downtrodden.

Muslims asylum seekers arrive in Europe like most others – as outsiders looking to find economic stability and opportunity, to live in peace and to reclaim their humanity. Most come from poor areas, war regions and situations of conflict. The refugee workshop at the Hope II Congress in 2011 identified several needs for working among asylum seekers in Europe such as: to overcome racism, discrimination and prejudice; to find welcoming places; to take a holistic approach; and to find common experiences. Apart from the complex administrative systems required to intervene in their lives, the concern for asylum seekers often stirs debates related to fundamental freedoms, human rights, detention, repatriation and non-refoulement.[3] Yet, more than this, God's concern for the nations lies at the heart hospitality.

Understanding Hospitality

In the Scriptures, hospitality involves spiritually significant encounters, often among strangers, as both guests and hosts who visit and welcome others into their lives and communities. In Genesis 19:1-29, Lot welcomes the two visitors to his city and takes them into his home for their protection. The towns people, on the other hand, reject the visitors from God and show their intent to abuse and mistreat them. In a controversial and often misunderstood show of hospitality, Lot pledges his daughters as assurance of his visitors' protection. In this early example of hospitality in the Scriptures, we already find the exchange of one person for the welfare of another person (v. 8). Lot's concern in his position of power was to treat his guests humanely and fairly. This is ultimately the example we see in God's own exchange of his Son's life for our life. Lot's welcome and effort to protect his guests ultimately saved him from impending destruction, demonstrating the mutuality and reciprocity in biblical hospitality.

Hospitality is significant because it not only shows the love of God for his people but it connects us to God's desire to save the nations. In 1 Kings 17:8-16, the widow of Zarepath reaches out to Elijah with all she has as he flees and hides from Ahab. As her guest, Elijah reciprocates the concern through the miracle of the flour bowl and oil jar[4] (v. 13-15). Likewise, Elisha would heal

---

[3] Triandafyllidou, A. *Irregular migration in Europe: myths and realities,* Farnham, England, Ashgate Pub. (2010), 28.

[4] 2 Kings 4:8-37 gives another example of God extending his mercy to the nations. The Shunammite woman reaches out to Elisha, who then shows compassion by asking what he can do for her. (v. 13) A lifelong friendship ensues and the prophet would eventually bring the woman's son back to life.

Namaan of leprosy (2 Kings 5:1-19). Unlike the King of Israel, who wanted nothing to do with the man, when Elisha hears, he invites Namaan to visit (v. 7-8). Eventually Namaan would be cured of his leprosy, profess the God of Israel (v. 15), and pledge his faithfulness (v. 17). These episodes of hospitality are so significant that as Jesus begins his own ministry, he not only proclaims his program for the poor, the captive, the blind and downtrodden (Luke 4:18-19), but he reminds the religious leaders that even in the days of Elijah and Elisha, God reached out to the nations[5] (Luke 4:25-27), and it happened through hospitality.

Several members from a local church once visited and mingled among undocumented asylum seekers waiting in line for food and assistance. They noticed a man full of tatoos, and looking more closely, they saw the words, "pray for me" tatooed along his arm. Like Namaan, covered with leprosy, this asylum seeker is also on a journey hoping that God is nearby. We cannot turn him away and we should surely respond differently from both the King of Israel and Jesus's own kinsmen(2 Kings 5:7; Luke 4:28-29).

The Scriptures are clear that, in loving and serving God, his people should love the stranger and the foreigner. "When a stranger sojourns with you in your land, you shall not do him wrong. You shall treat the stranger who sojourns with you as the native among you, and you shall love him as yourself, for you were strangers in the land of Egypt: I am the Lord your God" (Leviticus 19:33-34). Similarly, the two great commands of scripture instruct us in the love of God and the love of others (Matthew 22:34-40; Mark 12:28-31; Luke 10:27). Hospitality links these two commands together[6], and there are several highlights to remember about hospitality as we practice it among Muslim asylum seekers.

---

[5] Darrell Jackson points this out in his class notes on "Redemption and a missionary God." Jackson highlights the connection that Jesus makes between his ministry and that of the prophets. This underlines the reign of God across the whole of scripture. Jackson notes that this reign happens in hidden and frequently vulnerable ways. (pp. 4-5).

[6] Further examples of hospitality in the New Testament include: Matthew 25:31-40; Luke 11:5-10; Luke 14:12-24; Acts 10:23-33; Hebrwes 13:2; 1 Peter 4:9. In Hebrews 12:28-13:2, hospitality (v. 2) is in the context of God's grace for which we are thankful (v. 28) and our own love for others. Also in 1 Peter 4:8-9, in light of Christ's own love and suffering (1 Peter 4:1), Peter connects the word closely to the call for believers to love one another. Similarly, Romans 12:1-21 refers to hospitality as an example of genuine love that we show towards others.

Recognize others as fellow human beings

First, hospitality recognizes the least accepted people in society as fellow human beings. Too often we limit our recognition of the other and make the mistake of the lawyer in Luke 10:25-29. Having asked about salvation (v. 25), and wanting to justify what he has done to keep the commands for salvation (v. 29), the lawyer tries to make an issue out of the stranger. Jesus sees through this and tells the story of the good Samaritan. The story is not at all about the stranger but rather about the lawyer's own heart of mercy and the need to reach out to and welcome the stranger (v. 36-37).

It is easy to see the poverty and conflicts in other countries as a lack of competence to succeed or initiative to find solutions. The issues that drive asylum seekers onto our highways and into our lands are complex and dependent on many inter-related issues. Yet, there is the tendency in wealthy nations to mistake the presence of asylum seekers from other countries, who are different and poorer than we are, as a threat to our culture and as an effort on their part to get something for nothing. Showing great courage, determination and resourcefulness, often asylum seekers have exhausted their options and feel forced to take the steps they do. We would do much better to invest our energy and efforts to recognize these people and to share in what they might offer, rather than to exclude and separate them from ourselves.

Miroslav Volf points out that the exclusion of others should be based on an objective evil and not on our sinful preferences.[7] The mistake of the lawyer in Luke 10 is to make a preferential option about others based on his own sinful and misinformed ideas. Volf describes three common mistakes in recognizing others. First, we expect them to assimilate. Second, we dominate the relationship, and third we ignore the issues.[8] Applied to asylum seekers, we make these mistake by saying:

> "We'll accept you, if you first become like us."
>
> "You will succeed best if you stay in your place, and do things the way we think you should."
>
> "This is their problem and when they get it sorted out then we can get involved."
>
> Like we see in the rich young ruler, these mistakes reflect a deeper problem in the heart of the host.

---

[7] Volf, M. *Exclusion and Embrace: a theological exploration of identity, otherness, and reconciliation.* Nashville, Abingdon Press (1996), 71-75.
[8] Ibid., 75.

These kind of attitudes increase the distance between the host culture and the guest. Edward Said uses the picture of farmers who set up boundaries between themselves and their surroundings. The land beyond they call 'barbarian'; that land is 'theirs'. In this way, we make a dichotomy between ourselves and others. The thinking of Said, suggests the idea of 'Othering' to mean that our image of those different from us serves to promote the domination of one cultural system over another.[9]

When we relate to others in this way, the shortcoming and the failures we see in others strengthens our own sense of identity. Like the lawyer whom Jesus confronts, the guiding maxim for most people becomes, "We know who we are by who we are not." "We are not illegal or criminal, we are not radical and dangerous. We are not different like these others. We are normal and acceptable – not like these others."[10]

Emotional and politically charged labels such as 'illegal immigrants' and 'extremists' shape this kind of rhetoric that is rooted in conflict[11] and that leads to both the rejection and dysfunction of asylum seekers.[12] These conflicts and issues ultimately reflect the sin driven world that forces people to flee and seek asylum. For all its effort to form policies that address the challenges, states like those in the EU usually end up forcing the issues, along with the asylum seekers, to external borders and regions beyond. Incarceration and deportation is becoming the standard practice in the West for responding to those who are different from us. The tradition of hospitality, however, unpacks a Christian response to the questions and issues of 'Othering'. It allows us to recognise others first as fellow human beings and to answer the questions as Jesus did with the Lawyer in Luke 10. As Volf demonstrates, to embrace others and to make the distinctions that we need to make, we need a Christ-centered life over a self-centered one.[13]

After several members of a small evangelical church visited once among asylum seekers from central asia, one man commented, "This has made my soul soar. Please come back a hundred times, but at least come back one time." These

---

[9] Said, E.W. *Orientalism,* U.K., Routledge and Kegan Paul (1978), 227.
[10] Cohen, R. *Frontiers of Identity: the British and the Others,* London: New York, Longman (1994).
[11] de Ruiter, Bert (2010). *Sharing Lives.* Chapter 1 describes the difference between the Eurabia view of Islam and the Euro-Islam view. This is an example of rhetoric that is rooted in conflict. While the Euro-Islam view is more moderate, the Eurabia view is driven by fear and the belief that there is an inevitable clash of cultures.
[12] Cohen, 186. Zetter, R. "More labels, fewer refugees: Making and remaking the refugee label in an era of globalisation." Journal of Refugee Studies, 20, 172-192.
[13] Volf, 71

asylum seekers lived in an isolated house on the outskirts of the small village and another man said, "Why do you give us this gift? I have stayed here for three years and nobody has ever come to visit us!" To visit and befriend asylum seekers, such as these recognizes, them as fellow human beings and fills a vacuum in their souls. Jesus said, "I was hungry and you gave me food, I was thirsty and you gave me drink, I was a stranger and you visited me" (Matthew 25:35).

Offers a new basis for belonging

The film "Welcome" by French director, Phillipe Liorret (2009) portrays the divide between two worlds. The French context is all about the state law in regards to the asylum process and its prosecution, despite the inhumanity of this process. The context for the Kurdish asylum seeker is much bigger – a global human one in that he is driven by love for his girlfriend that he knew while in Iraq. Yet she is now in England, and he is stuck in Calais with no way to reach her except to swim across the channel. These two very different contexts illustrate the problematic situation in the asylum process. It is often a 'lose-lose' situation, with no way for those involved to reconcile or interact and both are doomed to fail. Hospitality has the ability to offer a new basis for belonging.

Belonging refers to the level of acceptance a person has as a result of the socialization process and the interaction between themselves and their community.[14] Membership in a political community is one kind of belonging, often formed by exclusion or inclusion on the basis of who a person is or not. The term 'sans papiers', referring to undocumented and unregistered asylum seekers in France, began in 1996 when 324 irregular migrants occupied a church in Paris on the basis of having no papers.[15] They had lost their identity and, through church asylum, appealed for a broader basis of political belonging.

In a similar way among asylum seekers, when we both visit and welcome them as visitors, we create a space for belonging that recognizes the way God cares for people and how Jesus interacts with others. These visits are built around our common humanity and they are rooted in God's own hospitality towards us. The ministry of Jesus is full of visits with others. While these hospitality situations are not the object of the gospel message, they become the means to show the mission of Jesus and to develop the purpose of God.[16]

---

[14] Richard, J. "The Socialist Tillich and Liberation Theology". in: Hellwig, M., Bulman, R.F. & Parrella, F.J. (eds) *Paul Tillich: a new Catholic assessment*. Collegeville, Minn. Liturgical Press (1994), 396).

[15] McNevin, A. "Political Belonging in a Neoliberal Ere: The Struggle of te Sans-Papiers." Citizenship Studies, 10, (2006), 135-151.

[16] Some examples of hospitality situations in which Jesus was both visited and welcomed others include: Matthew 10:1-6; Mark 1:29-31; Mark 2:1-2; Luke 4:40-41; Luke 5: 27-32; Luke 7:36-50; Luke 8:1-3; Luke 10:39-41; John 3:1-21; John 4:4-42.

Like many of those in Jesus' day, Muslim asylum seekers in Europe also need a renewed sense of belonging, especially in the face of a religious and cultural clash of values. They are on a collision course with an identity that is socially excluded and marginalized. The gap between themselves and EU society makes them susceptible to discrimination, unemployment and ultimately radicalization, with Islam becoming the unifying force.[17]

The EU recognizes the importance of dialogue for overcoming these kinds of challenges. The Radical Awareness Network (RAN) is one effort to counter the alienation and agenda of fringe groups in the EU. One of its aims is to bridge gaps through dialogue.[18] Similarly, in 2008, the EU dedicated the year to intercultural dialogue (ICD) as a way of strengthening a framework for open and respectful exchange and interaction between individuals, groups and organisations from different backgrounds and worldviews. The emphasis was not on a showcase of different cultures, but rather on the shared space between these cultures[19]. A recent communications from the EU Commission proposed "Five steps towards a more secure Europe."[20] One action point (p. 7) calls for the empowerment of ideas in the community that creates space for open debates to encourage credible role models and positive messages. The aim is to offer important alternative understandings and perspectives to the ones that enflame radicalism. Efforts by the EU to address the issues of asylum, such as the threat of radicalisation, also include a steady stream of directives for a common immigration and asylum policy. However, efforts like these to integrate Muslims into Europe often fail because they ignore a host of other relevant issues and particularly those related to religious identity.

The Christian idea and practice of hospitality is important for the EU, because it supports dialogue with those searching for belonging in another society. Hospitality is a fundamental expression of the Gospel message, rooted in the love of God and the love of others that leads to decisive involvement with others[21]. I once introduced a Kurdish friend to a man at my church. The two

---

[17] Anspaha, K. "The Integration of Islam in Europe: Preventing the radicalization of Muslim diasporas and counterterrorism policy." The ECPR Fourth Pan-European Conference on EU Politics. University of Latvia, Riga, Latvia: ECPR (2008), 6.

[18] "Preventing Radicalisation to Terrorism and Violent Extremism: Strenghtening the EU's Response". RAN Collection: Approaches, lessons learned and practices. Radical Awareness Network (2004), 38.

[19] "Sharing Diversity: National approaches to intercultural dialogue in Europe." European Institute for Comparative Cultural Research (2008), 11.

[20] "The EU Internal Security Strategy in Action: Five steps towards a more secure Europe." European Commission Home Affairs (2010).

[21] Bretherton L. "Tolerance, Education and Hospitality: A Theological Proposal." Studies in Christian Ethics (2004), 17, 25).

began to visit with each other and one day my Kurdish friend went to church while I was away. After the service they also gathered for a meal. Afterward, the Kurdish friend sent me the following SMS, "I went to the church. we sang, we prayed and we ate." This sums up the decisive and practical way that hospitality builds community and a sense of belonging.

Through hospitality we can speak to the physical, social and spiritual dimensions of persons, and in this way provide a framework for connecting theology to the Church's concern for issues like poverty, pain, suffering and inclusion of others[22]. This practice radically contrasts with the normal human tendency to treat outsiders and those different from us as un-welcomed guests and even non-humans who should be suspected and discriminated against[23]. Hospitality like Jesus practiced and received creates space where strangers find belonging and where enemies become allies, just as Jesus became friends with sinners.

Transforms and changes life

The possibility to address issues of belonging leads to a final important aspect of hospitality: it engages life in a practical way that can replace one set of values and understanding with another. Hospitality carries the potential to transform lives and perspectives, and in this way it lies at the centre of theology. Through hospitality, we connect with God's own journey in this world to restore his image and reconcile creation. Barth titled the first section of his volume on reconciliation, "The way of the son of God into the far country." Barth in his theology turns away from the humanist theology of his day to take a radical view of atonement centered around the Trinity and incarnation. He makes us aware of the nature and character of God as the humble Son of God who comes into the world as a reconciler and obedient servant. As one who goes to a far country, Christ leaves his own home in heaven to find a new one on earth. In terms of the world today, Christ comes as an asylum seeker who would be rejected. When we can grasp the magnitude of this, we can begin to understand the significance of our hospitality for those like Jesus, as well as the significance of Jesus' own words that say, when we visit those in prison, the needy and the stranger, we visit him (Matthew 25:34-40).

Situations of hospitality are about more than cozy visits and warm drinks – they are about transformation and seeing the world around us as God sees it. For example, the outcome of the visit among the asylum seekers outside the village was also transformational. Eventually the mayor, as well as the local Catholic

---

[22] Pohl, C.D. "Making Room: Recovering Hospitality as a Christian Tradition." Grand Rapids, Mich. W.B. Eerdmans (1999), 9.
[23] Denaux A. Studies in the Gospel of Luke: structure, language and theology. Berlin, Lit; London: Global (2011), 99.

church, saw the efforts of the small evangelical church. The efforts to visit and welcome the asylum seekers initiated dialogue about how the community could take part. As another mayor exagerated, "We do not want asylum seekers stranded in our fields and dieing in our streets." Most significantly, the small church became a viable and equal partner in the community.

This is like the widow's experience in welcoming and opening her life to Elijah (1 Kings 17:8-24). Hospitality potentially calls us to search our souls and to give up all we have hoped in. Similarly, we find this significance in the New Testament as well. One example is Peter's visit to Cornelius in Joppa, who had invited him to hear his message (Acts 10:23-48). The visit would prove transforming to both men, and indeed all of Christian theology, in regards to God's love for others beyond the Jewish nation.

Hospitality is anything but a casual and insignificant get together. Hospitality is the place and setting for the life giving work of God in our lives. Among Muslim asylum seekers, this service not only builds relationships rooted in genuine love (Romans 12:9-13), but it offers the chance to explore one of the important and most asked questions among every disillusioned, tired and struggling asylum seeker: "Now that I am here, and in light of all that I face, what will I do with my life?" These are questions that require trust, time and help to answer, and those that can transform our lives.

Practical concerns for welcoming and visiting asylum seekers

1. Plan a visit – Arrange a time and place to meet. Show how and where to go and offer to help with the transportation. Exchange phone numbers or other information in order to contact each other suddenly if needed.

2. Ideas – Take a walk; share a meal; look at photos; help with language needs.

3. Language barriers – Invite another person along to help with the conversation; plan an activity; watch a film in their language. Speak in simple clear sentences. Avoid unusual jargon or clichés.

4. Material help – It is possible that the asylum seeker will ask for help with financial, work or asylum matters. It is okay to say, "No." Try to understand what the need is. Offer to pray for the situation. Ask others on their behalf.

5. Faith matters – Be natural and genuine when you discuss faith issues. Invite, welcome and listen to their opinions. Avoid arguments.

6. Give hope – Asylum seekers face a lot of stress and uncertainty. When they share about these situations, invite them to speak freely. Your presence and listening ear has an important calming effect that can bring hope and encouragement. Offer to pray for the situation or to share a short scripture.

7. Find purpose – More than half of the asylum seekers in Europe will not receive asylum. They face rejection and the need to make new plans. Ask about their hopes and dreams and what the next steps are in their lives.

8. Prayer – Many asylum seekers understand the need for prayer. It builds solidarity with them and shows our dependence on God as human beings. Share about your prayers for them, and, when it is relevant and natural, offer to pray immediately. Give a short simple and genuine prayer.

9. Further Contact – It is easy to lose contact with asylum seekers. Phone numbers will expire or they may suddenly relocate or leave the country. Don't be surprised by these changes. Stay in touch through facebook, skype and current phone numbers.

Steps like these reflect both our effort to understand the issues of asylum seekers and to recognize them as fellow human beings. These steps are guided and informed by Jesus' own example in many situations of hospitality. Most of all, these situations offer the possibility to nurture needs of belonging that ultimately can transform our understanding and perspective of the world.

CHAPTER 8

Engaging through Dialogue

Ishak Ghatas

Introduction

Conflicts seem to have no geographical boundaries. In the European context, significant changes have led to the increasingly pluralistic, multi-faith Europe. Christian individuals as well as churches are challenged to relate to people from other faiths. Greater understanding of 'inter-faith dialogue and cooperation' is needed, since ignorance may lead to intolerance and conflict fueled by religion. Fundamentalism and radical beliefs may increase if 'the other' is seen as an enemy. Could dialogue be the first significant step to assess stable relationships?

In the interfaith dialogue two or more parties seek to express their views and listen respectfully to their counterparts and are willing to adjust one's own. Could developing different modes of dialogue attract involvements? Could interfaith dialogue, as a formal discussion aimed towards developing greater mutual understanding between different religious traditions, lead to better engagement with Muslims? The purpose of this chapter is to address engagement with Muslims through dialogue. Other relevant questions are:

i   Could a brief understanding of Muslims' presence in Europe and the development of mutual ideologies increase an awareness that enhances dialogue?

ii If there are basic and essential differences between Christianity and Islam, which cannot be ignored, are there also common elements which can be discussed. Could dialogue become the medium of authentic witness?

iii Practical considerations: how to connect with 'the other' in a common ground?

1. European context and the development of Islam

The history of Muslim in Europe

Muslims came to Europe for various reasons; some came as 'guest workers', students and others arrived as refugees or simply following countries of former colonialism. In the beginning, literature concerning Islam in Europe focussed more on Europe[1] than on Muslims but now more thought is given to the state of

---

[1] That is due to the fact that Muslims are not there to stay permanently and to the

Muslims in Europe. Muslims themselves, especially those of the second and third generation reflect on their permanent situation and on how to live as Europeans and Muslims who meet both moral obligations towards hosting countries and religious obligations towards Islam. It is significant that Muslims in Europe are diverse and some belong to the radical Islam movement.

Radical beliefs in Christianity and Islam might hinder dialogue. The Christian sense of superiority or reducing Islam to an 'anti-Christian' faith, may consider any dialogue unnecessary. Radical Muslims attempt to analyse events through faith. Radical Muslims emphasise 'comprehensive understanding of Jihad (holy/sacred war) and its application to nearly every aspect of human life. In this sense, it is necessary that Islam claims and preaches a political and a theocentric function, a political role, and that its social message and change are integral elements of its religious vision … The force of Islamic ideology, especially concerning holy war (Jihad), serves to create in radical Islamists a sense of Islamic universalism or 'globalism.'[2]

In the European context, both radical and the moderate Islam are present and will have an influential role in the future of Islam in Europe. 'On no issue is the Muslim and Western intellectual scene more divided or polarized than on the question of Islamic fundamentalism and its radical offshoots.'[3] Radicalism in Europe has its external roots but has been affected by European internal events. Both radical Islam and moderate Islam should be involved in the Christian-Muslim interfaith dialogue to enhance any future well-being in Europe.

2. Christian Muslim interfaith dialogue; its historical context and importance

Muslim-Christian interfaith dialogue dates back to early beginning of Islam. Islam includes awareness of biblical traditions that may invite dialogue[4]. Christians have attempted to explain and to defend theological issues contradicted in the texts of Islam[5].

---

concern to keep secular values. Recently, both Muslims and host countries pay more intention to get settled both 'Islam and Muslims'.

[2] Hassan, Gubara Said: *Europe and Radical Islam: Confrontation, Accommodation or Dialogue?* The Fifth Pan-European Conference. NL, The Hague, September 9-11, 2004, p. 7.

[3] Ibid., p. 4.

[4] The Qur'an includes positive and negative affirmation for Christianity. The writings of the Muslim scholar Ibn Taymīyah (d. 1328 A.C.) illustrate the point. In his book Al-jawāb al-ṣaḥīḥ li-man baddala dīn al-Masīḥ (The Correct Answer to Those Who Changed the Religion of Christ), Ibn Taymīyah collect the major theological and philosophical criticisms of Christianity.

[5] More details are mentioned in Mark Beaumont: *Christology in Dialogue with*

The two communities share geographical locations, values, and concerns since the dawn of Islam. 'While the Qur'an provides a framework for Muslims' understanding of Christians and Christianity, particular political, economic, and social considerations have shaped the encounter in each setting.'[6] On the Christian side, the rise of Islam in the seventh century presents many challenges. 'The arrival of Muslim rule in the traditionally Christian sectors ... brought a direct challenge to churches to give an account of the Christian faith especially that of Christ in the light of the Islamic understanding of him.'[7] Christians who were experts in the Arabic language led dialogue with Muslims using Islamic terminology to facilitate understanding.

The ninetieth and the twentieth centuries set the stage of organised interfaith dialogue. The Catholic Church and WCC (World Council of Churches) began significant efforts to set the stage for Christian-Muslim organised dialogue movement. Both the WCC and the Vatican initiated a number of meetings between Christian leaders and representatives of other religious traditions. In 1964, toward the end of the Second Ecumenical Council of the Vatican (Vatican II 1962-1965), Pope Paul VI established a Secretariat for Non-Christian Religions to study other religions. Pope John Paul II (1978-2005), was a strong advocate for the new approach to interfaith relations. The WCC established a new programme for Dialogue with People of Living Faiths and Ideologies (DFI) in 1971 with a primary focus on Muslim-Christian relations. The WCC and Vatican encouraged the publishing of books, articles, reports, working papers, and reviews by both Christians and Muslims[8]. Muslims are no longer people who live somewhere else; they are in Europe to stay.

In the EU, there is a significant emphasis on promoting formal dialogue and discussion between religious communities to foster more harmonious intercommunity relations. EU policy-makers encourage meetings with European

---

Muslims: A critical analysis of Christian presentations of Christ for Muslims from the Ninth and Twentieth Centuries. Regnum Books International: UK, 2011.

[6] "Muslim Christian Dialogue" in John L. Esposito ed.: *The Oxford Encyclopedia of the Islamic World.* Oxford University Press, pp. 182-187.

[7] See Mark Beaumont p. 12. In general some Christian leaders considered Islam as a Christian heresy while others went further to considers it as the anti-Christ. John of Damascus in the eighth century provided the first coherent treatment of Islam. For more details See Mark Beaumont pp. 12-18.

[8] See Current Dialogue. Geneva, 1980. Publication of the World Council of Churches, featuring articles, reports, reviews, and bibliographies. Encounter: Documents for Muslim-Christian Understanding. Rome, 1965. Publication of the Pontifical Council for Interreligious Dialogue. Sherwin, Byron L., and Harold Kasimow, eds. John Paul II and Interreligious Dialogue. Maryknoll, N.Y.: Orbis, 1999.

religions.⁹ It is important that other modes of dialogue should be considered. Dialogues including ordinary people, rather than only leaders, should be encouraged as well, including radical groups.

3. Outlying the usefulness of Inter-religious dialogue

Islam and the West 'reflect two distinct civilizational orders with their own specific understanding of the cosmos, social existence and the relations within it. However in a reaction to this 'civilizational clash', an inter-civilizational dialogue vision is receiving an increasing attention in both the Muslim and Western worlds.'[10] Dialogue provides the platform for people to acknowledge the contrast between the violence or clash of civilisation perpetrated and the ideals of peace and love.

Dialogue begins with understanding the other. Whether Christian interfaith dialogue is conducted with radicals or moderates, there is much in common between Islam and Christianity and much that is distinctively Islamic or Christian. It is worth noticing that other issues present a central controversy: 'the central controversy between Islam and Christianity has to do with the distancing or otherwise between the divine and the human. It is this which pervades all the themes of revelation, prophetic vocation, the ways of divine mercy, the categories of law and love, the degree of *kenosis* (or self-emptying) in creation itself on God's part, and the question of Jesus and the cross.'[11] Such issues need not be ignored and dialogue may help both parties in readiness to re-think thoughts and responses. Radical concepts in particular need to be considered in any interfaith dialogue. In order for the dialogue process to accomplish its aims, awareness of both the external and internal events that influence radicalism demand a careful analysis. 'Muslim-Christian encounters or relations have been overshadowed by neighbourhood rivalry, confrontation and conflicts over power, hearts and minds worldwide. This confrontation has involved such historical events as the defeat of the Christian Byzantine Empire by Islam in the seventh century; the fanatic polemic and brutal combats of the Crusades during the eleventh and twelfth centuries; the expulsion of Muslims from Spain in 1492, the creation of the State of Israel in 1948, and the current global resurgence and reassertion of Islam, including its radical brand or version.'[12] All these events affect Islamic worldviews and could be more visible in radical ideas. Dialogue provides access

---

[9] Leaders' European policy centre www;dialogue2008. (27.02.2014).

[10] Hassan (2004), p. 13.

[11] Badru D. Kateregga and David W. Shenk. 2000: "A Muslim and a Christian in Dialogue." *The World of Islam* – Resources for Understanding, Global Mapping International, p. 9.

[12] Hassan (2004), p. 12.

to windows of understanding of how others define their respective view. It is the first step toward accommodating or making space within oneself for the other in order to resolve such historical conflicts.

In order to accomplish maximum outcomes through dialogue, it is important that religious communities, rather than just scholars, talk to each other. Dialogue should not be confined to closed circles or groups of people; rather it should be opened to the public to help community members to be aware of the results that may occur of these dialogues. It is equally important to include all groups in dialogue, not just the main stream group.

4. Possibilities of engaging different groups in dialogue

One of the challenges of dialogue is to seek out and engage different groups, even though they may not represent the 'official' or mainstream Islam. It is common for one group to want to continue the dialogue with a partner that it feels comfortable talking with. This further perpetuates the conversation between dominant groups and alienates the voices of minority groups. Radical Islam is always present in European life and even more visible in public life. It could be the minority that controls the voice of the majority. Ignoring them is a mistake. Dialogue that fits their context is possible and is to be encouraged.

Radical Islam claims to be 'the conservative group' which might attract younger European. Much of its development came as a reaction to the internal challenges of modernity and the external influence due to Western involvement in Islamic countries. These issues should provide topics for dialogue. Dialogue can function as the outlet for any potential struggles. The other alternatives, which Europe has experienced are the attacks that seemed to provide the only possible outlets at the time to express anger over undesirable events. Dialogue may help as a mechanism to seek peaceful ways to settle conflicts. Serious and well prepared honest dialogue offers a better alternative.

European radical islamists discourse tries to convince Muslims to undertake *jihad* (peaceful or violent struggle) and to establish Islamic communities, Islamist forms of government and ultimately the Islamic European Empire. The intellectual sector of radical Islam can provide topics of dialogue that may help radicals as well as the moderates suppressed radical religious views and to seek other ways to accomplish the goals of the wider European communities.

Radicalism is not the product of religious crises alone; there are political, socio-economic, cultural local factors contribute to its growth. As a result: 'the new radical Islamic resurgence and revolt ... are not only directed against Western political hegemony, but also and primarily against the dominance of Western norms and values as well as against the world order they underpin.'[13]

---

[13] Hassan (2004), p. 25.

The struggle of radical Islam involves identity assentation. Different modes of dialogue over inter-civilization values should be included. Such issues open the eyes on what should be considered in order for dialogue to succeed. Dialogue with all groups of Muslims is important, possible and should be stimulated.

5. Conclusion

Dialogue presents challenges, but it is worth considering. The rise of Islam in Europe is a reality that should not neglected in any possible interfaith dialogue. Two extremes to be avoided in dealing with Islam in Europe include: playing down any significant place for dialogue with radicalism, or overlooking existing characteristic differences. Ignorance might lead to intolerance and eventually to possible clashes. Interfaith dialogue, with all groups represent in society, could build human dignity and security. The hope of present or future total affiliation or passive peaceful accommodation of all Muslim groups is not possible and should not be expected as an alternative to dialogue.

In general, the motives of dialogue include a 'desire to foster understanding, to stimulate communication, to correct stereotypes, to work on specific problems of mutual concern, to explore similarities and differences, and to facilitate means of witness and cooperation.'[14] True in any dialogue it is especially so for interfaith dialogue.

Christianity and Islam are the two largest faiths and pragmatic need for dialogue is particularly acute. In Europe, the way in which they relate to each other is bound to have profound implications. Both have radical groups that may not be equal in their influence, but both should be involved in any interfaith dialogue. One must learn to live his/her faith with integrity while respecting 'the other'.

Christianity (as well as Islam)[15] involves a missionary mandate to be in discussion and witness with others. In order to promote the inherent worth and dignity of every person, their spirituality as part of their traditions should be upheld. As 'the other' respects each individual's search for truth and meaning, he/she encourages the other's search journeys. As Christians work to build the kingdom of God, they need to learn and to relate the message in the context of the world's spiritual traditions. Muslims as well must seek peaceful means to accomplish their given task. All of these considerations that we covenant to affirm and to promote must encourage us to speak with one another in a spirit of dialogue.

---

[14] Mevlev-Russia, p. 181.

[15] The Islamic mandate 'dawah' or calling people to Islam is the equivalent to the Christian missionary mandate.

Christians should see Muslims are a part of their European local communities. Muslims' struggles deserve Christian involvements. Both radical and moderate Muslims have the right to hear and to experience the Christian message. Dialogue could present an active practical channel.

6. Practical remarks

i. The Interfaith dialogue[16] respects diversity, explores others beliefs and traditions and accept them as valuable resources. It refers to cooperative and positive interaction between people that defines a greater mutual understanding of their different religious traditions. In this context, it is important to note that the word 'dialogue' refers to the act of seeing through and should empower one to 'see through' the faith of the other.

ii. The process of self-definition, in the course of dialogue, requires each group to express itself based on its own terms and for the partner in dialogue to accept and respect that context of self-definition. Interfaith dialogue must enable re-examining 'false assumptions' of the other based on the one's self-definition.

iii. It should be understood that interfaith dialogue is generally favoured by academics but often suffers from, civic/political development, local/international conflicts. The fear of European demographic changes in favour of Islam and the phenomena of radical fundamentalism should not limit or discourage dialogue.

iv. The interfaith dialogue does not promote the joining of religions, but refers to the cooperative and positive interactions between people of different religious and spiritual traditions. It is distinct from syncretism or alternative religion, in that dialogue often involves promoting understanding to increase acceptance of 'the other'.

v. It is not to promote one religion as being the true faith while the others are false, but its common goal is to create a peaceful and prosperous civilization. It involves mutual respect achieved through learning about and respecting diversity while appreciating the uniqueness of others.

vi. An essential component in dialogue is the willingness to re-examine one's assumptions of 'the others' in the light of how the others relate to their tradition. It expects the ability to strengthen or to adjust one's own engagement and interaction based on the experiences of the other.

---

[16] The word 'dialogue' comes from διάλογος; the prefix διά means through, by, among, and λόγος: word, reason, verb.

vii. One of the challenges of interfaith dialogue is to seek out and engage different groups, even though those who may not represent the 'official' or mainstream religious groups. It is common for one group to want and to continue the dialogue with a partner that it feels comfortable talking to. This may further conversation between dominant groups but it alienates the voices of minority groups that may be active and influential. In this context, active dialogue is to seek out and engage different groups, even radicals who may not represent the 'official' or mainstream body.

CHAPTER 9

Engaging Through Holistic Ministry

Hany Girgis

Introduction

Throughout most of my life, I have been a man of books, ideals, and theories. I believed, and still believe, that all people have the right to understand God's word, plans, and ideas, in the context of their own worldview. Achieving this target is the ongoing task of many scholars and teachers, who seek to creatively reinterpret the word of God to make sense of it for people in their own cultural context. This goal I had in mind when I started our ministry to Muslim immigrants in Europe. I tried to carry on this task faithfully, yet the results in the first couple of years were discouraging. I remember one experience that took place when I was trying to organize what I thought was a creative, evangelistic event. To promote it, I recruited a group of volunteers and we set out daily for a whole week to invite people to our event. Between our team, we spent a total of 400 hours on the streets, talking to people and encouraging them to come. On top of that, we spent many hours carrying out logistic and administrative work in preparation. When the day finally came, we had only one person, who showed up one hour late. It was incredibly frustrating.

A few weeks later, my wife invited a couple of Muslim women she had met at our son's school to come for tea. During their visit, they overheard her speaking in English on the phone and asked her if she could teach the language to their children. In a week or so, the kids asked if they could invite their friends as well, and the word spread. Soon the informal language class grew to include computer classes. In a few weeks, we had eleven people coming regularly to our home, including teenagers and young adults.

We did the math: 400 hours a week = 1 person compared to: 8 hours a week = 11 people

We recognized that something different happened the second time around: we had hit the right button. We asked ourselves how we could repeat this. Through this experience, we were introduced to holistic ministry, born out of the practical needs of the people we were reaching.

The unique role of Holistic Ministry in serving Muslim immigrants

Holistic ministry can be defined as ministry that serves people in multiple dimensions, by presenting the Gospel not just in words but also deeds by providing for the spiritual, emotional, and physical needs of a community. Holistic ministries are not new in Europe but are widespread and address many social needs. Programs aimed at education, sports, legal support, artistic expression, youth clubs and psychological support, are some of initiatives undertaken. Holistic ministry is in its golden era, as only several decades ago it was either being rebuked for preaching the 'Social Gospel'[1] or being charged with compromising on evangelism[2].

This type of ministry plays an important role in church life and the community surrounding it. Besides, holistic ministry has particular importance in Muslim immigrant ministry. The first part of this chapter highlights this unique role.

Holistic ministry: an entrance to the Muslim community

The modern mission towards Muslims began around the end of the 18th century, when missionaries sought ways to reach out to Muslims. Several years of research and experimentation led to a list of the most effective areas of ministry, which was presented in a conference titled "Mission Work Among Muslims" in Cairo, in 1906. The list included the main opportunities for effective ministry: first, medical work; second, distributing literature; third, Christian education; and finally, relational work among women[3].

From the very beginning, holistic ministries were an essential reality for the work amongst Muslims. In seeking entrance to the Muslim community, missionaries considered the practical needs of people, and ministered via medical and educational services.

This way of introducing ministry is equally relevant to immigrant communities in Europe, as they have a variety of needs in their new society. Governments and charities actively try to respond to these needs; however, it is the way the service is presented, and the amount of care shown, that makes people accept

---

[1] By the beginning of the 20th century many evangelicals sought to reinterpret the Bible from a more modern point of view about mission work. The idea was that we had progressed beyond the belief in supernatural phenomena; therefore, they focused on offering social services and left out all talk about heaven, hell, conversion and other spiritual reality. This reconstructed version of Christian mission became known as the Social Gospel, which considered by many as a substitute for evangelism. Rusel, M. (2008) *Christian mission: are we on a slippery slope? Christian mission is holistic.* International Journal of Frontier Missiology 25:2 Summer 2008. Available online from: http://www.ijfm.org/PDFs_IJFM/25_2_PDFs/Russell.pdf.

[2] Samuel, V., & Sugden, C. (1987). *The Church in response to human need.* Grand Rapids, Mich, W.B. Eerdmans Pub. Co.

[3] Richter, J. (1910). *A history of Protestant missions in the Near East.* New York, Fleming H. Revell.

it. When Christians present their services with cultural sensitivity and the right motives, the immigrant community receives it with deep appreciation. This is what gives Christians an entrance to and a place in the immigrant community.

Knowing each other

Holistic ministries play a unique role in engaging with Muslim immigrants in Europe, mainly because of their particular perception and ideas about Christians and Christianity. The majority of Muslims not only believe that Christianity holds to different theological and doctrinal positions[4], but also, as Muslims, they cannot possibly imagine themselves living the same way that 'Christians' are living. They have cultivated distorted ideas about the lifestyle, culture and moral standards of Christians, confusing it with secular European lifestyles[5]. For many of them, Christianity and the West are the same thing; when they compare 'ideal' Islam with the immorality they observe in Europe, it confirms to them that Islam is superior and that Christianity has nothing to offer. For this reason, amongst others, Muslims are living in an isolated world[6]. Walls of prejudice, fortified by anti-Europeanization Islamic ideas, are separating them from the community around them[7].

Christians also have their fears and suspicions fueled by many negative images in the media. They feel crippled in drawing near to Muslims, unable to initiate spiritual dialogue[8]. To a great extent, both sides are convinced that there is neither possibility nor reason to create and maintain relationships. Holistic ministry provides a neutral ground where both sides are able to get to know each other at a personal level. This is possible when there are genuine initiatives to care for people, and good intentions to understand them personally.

Changing perception

Despite the fact that holistic ministry does not immediately respond to Islamic doctrinal questions, for many Muslims it facilitates a firsthand experience of Christians' lifestyle and materializes before them the meaning of Christianity. This is a vital factor in the process of interacting with Muslim immigrants, be-

---

[4] Ayoub, M., & Omar, I. A. (2007). *A Muslim view of Christianity: essays on dialogue*. Maryknoll, N.Y., Orbis Books. pp. 212-229.

[5] Schirrmacher, C. (2008). *Islam and society: sharia law – jihad – women in Islam*; essays. Bonn, Verl. für Kultur und Wiss. p. 64.

[6] Institute for the Study of Islam and Christianity. (2005). *Islam in Britain: the British Muslim community in February 2005*. Pewsey, Isaac Pub. pp. 38-43.

[7] Abicht, L. (2008). *Islam & Europe: Challenges and Opportunities*. Belgium, Leuven University Press. pp. 60-61.

[8] De Ruiter, Bert (2010). *Sharing Lives: Overcoming Our Fear of Islam*. Nürnberg, VTR. pp. 39-59.

cause the changing of perceptions of God and Christianity takes place in those personal interactions. This is confirmed by studies[9], and the witness of many converted Muslims, who came to know the Gospel through a journey with Christian friends[10].

Many Muslims are not just lacking knowledge about the real meaning of the gospel; the majority also holds very negative ideas and perceptions about Christianity which prevent them from imagining any possible situation where they would consider the message of the Gospel as an option for their personal life[11]. Many strongly maintain this position, despite the lack of rational argument for the superiority of their Islamic ideology. I have personally met hundreds of Muslims who have held such negative perceptions and consider Christianity unacceptable according to their cultural and moral standards[12]. Some may think that informing them accurately about Christianity would change this perception. However, this is made difficult due to high rates of illiteracy in such communities where the practice of critical appraisal and personal research are uncommon. Where informative Christian media exists, they are easily blocked (save some satellite broadcasting channels) by community gate-keepers, such as the mosque leaders or Islamic organisations. Some churches and ministries reaching out through book tables or free distribution of printed materials have reported that Muslim leaders would immediately forbid their community from receiving it and, in some cases, issue strong warnings about interacting with Christians at all. Thus, though there is some distribution that is taking place in various locations, the religious dialogue, which is hoped for after the distribution, happens mostly on the level of the leadership, and not at street level. That leaves the vast majority of Muslim immigrants with no real experience of understanding the meaning of Christian teaching.

---

[9] One of the most popular theories, which has been supported by most sociological studies of conversion done thus far, focusing mainly on people who joined NRM's in the United States, is that people convert along relationship lines. This theory explains both the why and the how of conversion by following people's affective ties. The main argument is that when people's relationships with members of a new religious group become more significant, to the point that they outweigh their affiliations with previous relationships, that is when they will choose to affiliate to a new religion (Kraft, K. A. 2007). pp. 101-102.

[10] Kraft, K. A. (2007). Community and identity among Arabs of a Muslim background who choose to follow a Christian faith. Bristol, University of Bristol. pp. 101-102.

[11] ATA, I. W. (2009). *Us and Them Muslim-Christian Relations and Cultural Harmony in Australia*. Bowen Hills, Australian Academic Press. pp. 11-12.

[12] Sennels, N. (2010) *Muslims and Westerners: The Psychological Differences*. Book review, available online: http://www.newenglishreview.org/Nicolai_Sennels/Muslims _and_Westerners%3A__The_Psychological_Differences.

Many converted Muslims have shared that their change of perception happened over time through a process where exposure and observation were allowed, questions were asked and conclusions were eventually drawn out and compared with previous ways of thinking. This process has been confirmed in several studies of conversion: it is usually a process involving many small steps. It starts with one motivation, and leads to other motives.[13] This process is not necessarily organized in a logical sequence or ordered steps; rather it is like filling in missing pieces of a puzzle or changing the place of the pieces to make the picture clearer. Holistic ministries provide ample time necessary for this to take place. Without this time and the lively personal interaction, it would be difficult for a large sector of Muslim immigrants – especially those who are illiterate or have a low level of education – to have the chance to reconsider perceptions or change strongly held positions.

Secured space to explore

Holistic ministry, particulary among Muslims, allows them a safe space for exploring the meaning and practices of spiritual life. As I mentioned in the introduction, we have tried many ways to invite Muslims to attend events that preach the Gospel. Despite initial interest and curiosity at first contact, hardly any of them showed up. Over time we discovered that one reason was fear of consequences, i.e. someone from their community would identify them and expose them[14]. Even though many of these events were not held in a church building, the fact that a Christian issue would be discussed was enough to provoke this kind of fear in many interested people. Often, the interested persons faced confrontation or accusations from family and friends. In one case, a person received a phone call from his father in North Africa, the day after attending one of our events, telling him that he heard from some friends that his son is joining Christians in their meetings.

A major advantage that holistic ministry offers is a safe haven from Muslim community backlashes; this applies for both Christian workers and interested Muslims. Interested persons need, and really appreciate, the opportunity to observe, ask questions whenever they like, and take some small steps to try the type of life they observe without feeling of the burden of a watching community.

---

[13] Maurer, A. (1999). *In search of a new life: conversion motives of Christians and Muslims.* [S.l.], [s.n].

Kraft, K. A. (2012). *Searching for heaven in the real world: a sociological discussion of conversion in the Arab world.* Oxford, England, Regnum.

[14] Schantz, B. (1993). *Islam in Europe: Threat or Challenge to Christianity?.* Missiology: An International Review, 21(4), pp. 443-454. Available online from: http://mis.sagepub.com/content/21/4/443.full.pdf+html.

How to start and continue

Many existing holistic ministries have some Muslim immigrants as beneficiaries, while others wish to create new ministries specifically for this needy community. However, such ministry encounters practical questions, like: How do we start? How do we invite Muslims? What about the language barrier? To what extent, and when, should the Gospel be shared? They need to give answers to the questions of their churches and supporters, such as: Why does it take a lot of time and resources to share the gospel? Why is the Gospel shared in small pieces? Does this compromise its full meaning? Europe is the land of free speech, so why not just share all the truth? Yes, immigrants have many needs, but their true, and deepest need is for the gospel – shouldn't we give it to them first?. These valid and practical questions impose themselves on the reality of any vision to start a holistic ministry for Muslim immigrants.

In the following section I outline a model of a holistic ministry setting and its dynamics, that may facilitate answers to these questions. This model can be illustrated as follows:

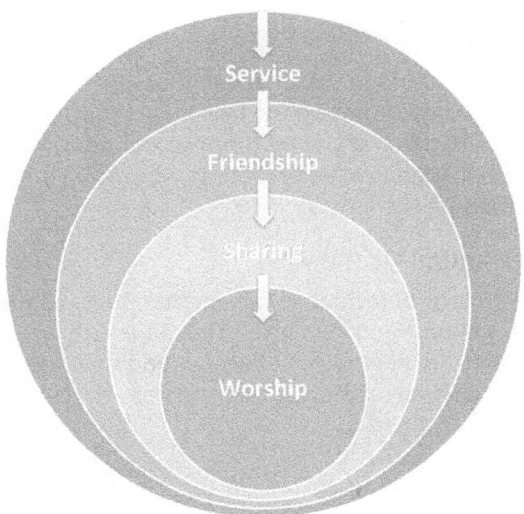

Before we discuss the meaning of each nested circle in the model, it is helpful to highlight some points:
- The model is derived from the experiences of many ministries in Europe. Not all of them necessarily follow all the finer details, but the main components have been experienced by many in the field.

- It is important to bear in mind that this model is based on the idea of Preparatory Work[15], which respects the time that Muslims need and process they go through to reach the point of adopting the Christian life paradigm.
- Each circle of the model has its own aims, dynamics and limitations. Moving to the next inner circle does not happen suddenly or automatically, but through sensitive and careful intentional effort. It is important to be discerning of the nature of the beneficiary group's needs and the degree of their openness to the Gospel.

Service Circle

The outer circle represents the type of service that the ministry should offer – the door to enter into the community. The nature of the service is normally decided by the observed, or researched, needs of the community, and the abilities of the volunteers in the ministry. There are many groups with different needs and sectors: women with similar needs, second generation immigrants, age-specific groups, different educational levels, etc. Once identified, the ministry can then tailor its services, and its Gospel presentation at a later stage; thus, becoming more effective at achieving its goals.

In this wide circle, workers have found that consistently meeting needs in suitable ways, is the most important factor in winning the trust of the beneficiaries. This is essential in allowing them to consider the workers as not just social workers, but friends are available to them. We will discuss this in more detail in the following sections.

Service Circle and ethical issues

One ethical argument objects that it is unacceptable to use people's needs to impose the Gospel on them[16]. I agree. Thus, it is critical to be informed about the realities of holistic ministries in Europe, and how workers can develop the Gospel presentation whilst offering their services to the community.

---

[15] Preparatory Work, or Pre-evangelistic Work as some call it, is using the acceptable and amiable ways to pave a ground to share gradually the full Message of the gospel. It aims to communicate the points of view of Christianity, and the logic behind it, on a certain topic or issue without asking the audience to make a decision or to take action as a result of hearing it right away. It allows the person having the needed time to process what is heard, before moving to the next step.

[16] Sherwood, D. (2002) *Ethical Integration Of Faith And Social Work Practice*. Nacsw's Journal, Social Work and Christianity. Vol. 29 (1). Available online from: http://www.nacsw.org/Download/CSW/Evangelism2.pdf.

Firstly there is no scarcity of social work in Europe. All the services Christians are already offered by governments with more resources and sometimes better presentation. Many charities, including Islamic ones, do the same. There is no monopoly, which means beneficiaries have options. Muslims who chose to go to Christian services do so because they feel appreciated, understood culturally, or treated well. This finding has been reported over and over again from different ministries.

Secondly, in most cases it is not practical to present any type of Christian message, preparatory or evangelistic, while carrying out the services or running activities. Ministries prepare separate such programs or events before or after the activities or on a different day. That leaves beneficiaries free to accept or reject the invitation to attend. Many holistic ministries report that when an invitation to a Christian program is offered, only some of their Muslim beneficiaries choose to attend. Hence, within the Service Circle, discussing religious issues or spirituality usually happens in a certain context of either close friendship, or special events, which we will discuss in the coming points.

Friendship Circle

Experienced workers in holistic ministry provide a context of trust and security, which many immigrants report is missing outside of their homeland[17]. Even though many Muslim immigrants express that their desire to experience a life free of the censorship and control experienced in their family and communities, is one reason for migrating, many actually miss the warmth and closeness of their former social network. Despite being 'controlling', their native community provided consistent support, assuming responsibility of the needs of its members. Many immigrants took this aspect of life for granted, failing to appreciate it until it was lost. Finding a group of people who practices these values of consistent support and close relationship, becomes a beautiful surprise for many, especially in the European context that can often feel very individualistic and impersonal. Establishing this friendly context in the ministry makes sharing lives, and the exchange of ideas and personal views, a spontaneous act, as a sense of mutual trust is built.

In practical terms, friendship in the context of holistic ministry represents time that workers and beneficiaries are spending together outside the scheduled activities of the service provided. This time is mostly spent talking about gen-

---

[17] Joseph, S., & Najamabadi, A. (2003). *Encyclopedia of women & Islamic cultures*. Leiden, Brill. Vol. 3, p. 202.
Grillo, R. D. (2008). *The family in question immigrant and ethnic minorities in multicultural Europe*. [Amsterdam], Amsterdam Univ. Press. Available online from: http://site.ebrary.com/id/10302669.

eral issues in life, sharing meals, and/or socializing in any common activity. The closeness of relationship removes all kinds of prejudices and defensiveness, uncovering the real persons and their needs. Hence, the religious dialogue is between two people, not two ideologies. Through this, it is possible for the Word of God to penetrate the heart, answer those needs and transform life.

Sharing Circle

For many Christian workers, sharing one's faith with others is the ultimate goal. Sharing the message in the context of holistic ministries mainly happens through two ways: personal sharing and organized events.

Personal sharing: As mentioned in the previous point, holistic ministries provide a variety of opportunities to know the people we serve personally. Through understanding the immigrant's personal needs, struggles, hopes, fears, moral and cultural dilemmas, and concerns for the future, the worker can present the message of the Gospel as a way of providing answers to such personal situations. This sensitivity allows for the presentation of the Gospel as a literal, personal message from God to the person, not merely a generalized belief. In those pivotal moments, when the person receives the message as an option for life, they cease focusing on the doctrinal differences between Islam and Christianity. They receive it as an answer from heaven to a personal struggle, though they may not know exactly how to handle it. Many workers have found that, in such moments, when they offered to pray for the person, to asking the Lord to intervene in the course of a life, friends eagerly welcomed it. The results of such encounters have always been tremendously life-changing.

Organized events: Most of these events are based on using the local calendar of feasts and celebrations. The events are organized to express the Christian point of view about the real meaning of the feast or the celebration, such as Christmas, Easter, Valentine's Day, etc. Some ministries use additional celebrations, such as a graduation ceremony of a course they have been offering, for the same purpose.

The content of the message shared in these events varies from preparatory messages to evangelistic preaching. This depends on the beneficiaries, the degree of their openness, and their relationship with the workers. In some cases, relationships are strong enough to allow for the running of workshops, seminars, or retreats, where some topics of interest are studied and discussed in depth, i.e. marital relationships, raising children, women's role in the community, cross-cultural marriages, third-culture kids issues, etc. All these events are presented with appropriate adaptation to fit the needs of listeners.

Worship (experience the presence of God)

Experiencing the presence of God transforms a person's life. Many Muslims recount this fact in testimonies. Seeking intentionally to expose them to this experience, when the context of trust is established, is highly recommended by almost all workers in holistic ministries. This could happen through inviting people who are open to join a church meeting or a celebration. The impact of exposure to worship, praise and singing, will often help Muslims to make sense of Christianity and its essence. Many of them report feeling something real and genuine penetrating their soul, giving them a sense of the presence of God. That does not mean necessarily that they have accepted or embraced Christianity in that moment. However they have recognized God in the encounter and acknowledged His presence, and have begun to realize how this may changes their lives. When they experience such a moment, it makes all the time invested in their journey worth it.

Holistic ministry is a long-term effort because moving with a person from one circle to the next can take a long time. However, its layers of effect, which accumulate slowly, are not easily erased. Whether the worker sees a lasting change or not, these layers of changed perception lay an important foundation, waiting for someone else to continue building. The effort of love never fails.

CHAPTER 10

Engaging with Other Believers – Establishing Networks

Bryan Knell

We are living at a very exciting time in the history of the world. The Christian community is growing faster than ever. Europe would certainly not be promoted as an example of that growth but, while Christendom and the vestiges of formal religion may be in decline, vibrant Christianity is growing. Young followers of Jesus are coming together and forming churches in many countries. The number of Muslims in Europe may be increasing, but Islam is facing huge challenges today, both internally and in the way it presents itself to the world. An increasing number of Europeans from a Muslim background are following Jesus.

Many new expressions of Christian commitment are not linked to established denominations, but come together in informal networks or stay staunchly independent. Even some of those linked to established denominations are forming new networks to engage with Muslims.

Now is the time to recognise what God is doing among us in Europe, to rejoice in all that is happening and to make sure that we are ready to work together to see our continent changed through the power of the Holy Spirit. This chapter insists that, whatever the difficulties, inclinations of our own personalities, or differences of opinion, we must not forge an independent path and ignore the ministry of others.

In the UK we have developed a network that has had some success in bringing together many people holding different beliefs and opinions who are involved in Muslim ministry. CRIB (Christian responses to Islam in Britain) started in 1998. It is not perfect; it does not have all the answers; it is keen to learn from others, and there will be struggles ahead; but we are committed to recognising and respecting each other. CRIB involves about 700 people, most of whom are part of other denominational, organisational or city-based networks. CRIB could be described as a network of networks and individuals.

In this chapter, we are going to look at Jesus' plea for unity, what it means to build respect and what gets in the way of our working together. There are things we can learn from the CRIB experience, and we will examine how to deal with disagreements that will inevitably come.

Unity ...

We must start with the words of Jesus. Just before Jesus went through the incredible physical and mental torture and subsequent death that made our forgiveness and acceptance by the Father possible, He prayed for us. It is difficult to imagine an occasion or situation when Jesus' concern for us would be clearer in his mind and in the words he said to the Father.

"My prayer is not for them (his original followers) alone. I pray also for those who will believe in me through their message, that all of them may be one, Father, just as you are in me and I am in you. May they also be in us so that the world may believe that you have sent me. I have given them the glory that you gave me, that they may be one as we are one: I in them and you in me. May they be brought to complete unity to let the world know that you sent me and have loved them even as you have loved me." (John 17:20-23)

Jesus' concern is obviously for our unity, but it is not that we may have a good time together, or that we would grow and develop as committed disciples of Jesus, or even that God would be able to rejoice as we mirror the unity of the Godhead. Rather this oneness that Jesus prayed to the Father for was so that the world would see and believe. This point comes out twice in just three verses with these words: "that the world may believe", and "to let the world know".

The biggest barrier to the proclamation of the Kingdom – and the greatest hindrance to people responding to the gospel – is disunity and squabbling amongst Christians. This has always been the case, but it is more obvious and destructive today because easier communication means that disagreements are more public and people can take sides and spread false information so readily.

What comes through as the highest priority on Jesus' agenda when He thinks of us is supported by Paul, who asked the Philippians (and us) to "make my joy complete by being like-minded, having the same love, being one in spirit and purpose" (Philippians 2:2). To the Romans he wrote, "If it is possible, as far as it depends on you, live at peace with everyone" (Romans 12:18), and "Let us therefore make every effort to do what leads to peace and to mutual edification" (Romans 14:19).

... not uniformity

God made us all wonderfully different. He gave us different backgrounds, different levels of intelligence, different personalities, different personal preferences and different abilities to understand his truth. That diversity should be celebrated among us and we should rejoice at any opportunity to interact with someone different from ourselves who loves the Lord.

We do not all have to form one team, or all do things in the same way. There is plenty of opportunity for diversity and difference of approach and opinion, but God did not design us to be loners. Members of the Body of Christ are not to be independent, but inter-dependent. God's plan is that our unity will proclaim the gospel.[1]

We need to see networks of people engaging with Muslims established across Europe – national networks, different sorts of ministry networks, different church networks – and then make sure that those networks do, in fact, network together, keep in contact and talk to each other. We are not expecting Christians in ministry to Muslims to do the same things, to work on the same projects together or even to believe the same things about ministry methods, but we do believe that to walk away from others, to shun their fellowship, to demonise their methods or to sabotage their ministries brings shame on the Kingdom of God and pain to the heart of our Father God.

It has been said that church unity is very easy: you just get rid of all the people who disagree with you. Unfortunately, many churches seem to operate on that principle. Church leaders who feel threatened draw around them people who will agree with them and who won't rock the boat. The result is a church which must bring great sadness to Jesus.

Building respect

We are called to love and respect our brothers and sisters, not necessarily to agree with them. Respect is key: we are called upon in the New Testament to respect non-believers with whom we will inevitably disagree over the most basic things. The key verse about apologetics makes this clear: "But in your hearts set apart Christ as Lord. Always be prepared to give an answer to everyone who asks you to give the reason for the hope that you have. But do this with gentleness and respect" (1 Peter 3:15). In the previous chapter, we are told to show respect to everyone (1 Peter 2:17).

If respect is a basic Christian response to those outside the faith, it should certainly be the correct response to those with whom we share the fundamentals of the gospel.

CRIB has no doctrinal statement, no constitution, no by-laws and no manual of beliefs and practices, but it does have a mission statement. I believe that the centrality of this mission statement, and the way that we have read and mentioned it again and again, is the main reason why CRIB has stayed together in the hotly contested arena of Muslim ministry. It reads as follows:

---

[1] To read more about this: Alexander Strauch, *If you bite and devour one another – Biblical Principles for Handling Conflict.* Authentic Copyright, 2011.

CRIB is a network for evangelical Christians who are involved in all aspects of engagement with Muslims and Islam in Britain with the following goals.

1. *To provide an opportunity for regular meeting, networking and sharing of ideas and resources.*
2. *To foster mutual respect and unity among Christians.*
3. *To develop credible strategies for the church in responding to Islam in this country.*

I can say to many of my CRIB friends that I disagree with them and think they are wrong on a particular issue, but I still respect them. On occasions, I may have no alternative but to let people know that I disagree with them, but it will not be my intention to criticise them personally, nor to suggest that they have not carefully considered their approach, to speak against them or to denigrate their ministry, nor to sabotage their ministry. I will make every effort to love them as a Christian friend and will try to pray for them.

So why do we find it so difficult?

There are several reasons:

- Christians are often not good at disagreeing with each other. Maybe this is because we are too 'nice', or not honest enough, or fail to "speak the truth in love" as we are exhorted to in Ephesians 4. For a mixture of these reasons and others, we want to ignore, hush up or deny any disagreement. We behave as if we think Christian unity works because we all become programmed like a group of robots when we follow Christ. So we avoid disagreement whenever possible.

- Mission partners in pioneer situations are inevitably strong-minded, strong-willed and task-orientated people. That is what makes them effective in mission ... and often makes them difficult to work with.

- Engaging with Muslims is often highly charged emotionally. Islam challenges the Christian at the depths of his faith on things like the person of Jesus and the centrality of the cross. Asking a Muslim to change their allegiance and become a follower of Jesus could well mean that we are asking them to sign their own death warrant, or at least to sign away their job prospects, their inheritance and their marriage opportunities. No one can make such demands on another lightly.

- Seeking unity can seem to be a distraction. We could do without the stresses. The result of conflicts and different opinions is that many Christians give up on the hassle of trying to work with others and become independent: "I can't be bothered with all that, I just want to share Jesus with Muslims" is a common reaction.

It is pertinent to remember that one of the reasons why Islam emerged was because the Middle East faced a spiritual vacuum and turmoil which was the result of vicious debates within the Christian Church.

Learning from the CRIB experience

CRIB is an ongoing attempt to establish a network of evangelical Christians in the UK who will recognise and support each other. We still have much to learn, but we have had some success and pass on ideas for others who wish to establish networks for Muslim ministry throughout Europe.

1 Don't try to do too much

The more you try to do, the more there will be to disagree about. Limit what you do to a few clear statements and emphasise constantly the things that you are committed to and that draw you together. Don't specify HOW you are going to do things; allow people in the network to work that out as they go along and as they share together.

CRIB is NOT trying to be any of the following:
- An organization or a new agency.
- A group of people who agree about everything.
- Antagonistic towards those with other approaches to Muslims.
- A Christian uniformity.
- A programme of events.
- A motivating, mobilizing, training, mentoring, empowering or suchlike organisation. Many people in CRIB will be concentrating on these things in different ways, but they are not on CRIB's mandate.

Because we are committed only to our mission statement, we prevent ourselves from setting up accepted patterns of belief or practice. We are simply trying to achieve:
- A network of Muslim ministry specialists.
- A friendly community that understands the challenges involved.
- An antidote to ministry loneliness.
- A group sharing experiences and resources.
- A respect for others with differing views.
- A forum to develop workable strategies.
- An atmosphere that will encourage and enable Christians to work together.

2 Try to be as inclusive as possible

CRIB is not exclusive, but inclusive. We try to draw people together, to concentrate on those things that unite us and to rejoice in diversity. I estimate that over 80% of evangelical Christians involved in Muslim ministry in the UK would be happy to be part of CRIB. CRIB is overseen by a small committee which represents wide range of practitioners with different opinions.

At each end of the spectrum, there are those who exclude themselves. There are some in the UK who create a hostility towards Islam by what they say and write that breeds a fear in the minds and hearts of Christians. They use statistics irresponsibly, collect sensational statements by Muslims and proclaim the actions of extreme Muslims in the same way that the popular press does in order to create a fear that discourages any engagement with ordinary Muslims.

At the other end of the spectrum are those who see no challenge from the Muslim community, who believe that there is no need to evangelise Muslims because Islam can provide all the spiritual help they need.

Christians at both of these extremes would be uncomfortable in CRIB. Our mission statement says that we are a 'network for evangelical Christians ...' We have welcomed non-evangelical Christians to our events, but on the understanding that we operate from certain unspecified assumptions that are taken for granted and are not up for discussion. We are thinking about issues like acceptance with God as only possible through Jesus Christ, that sharing the gospel with Muslims is an essential responsibility and that the Bible is our authority in faith and conduct.

3 Try to be objective

This is a big ask, as people get very wound up about Islam because it challenges not only the truths of the biblical revelation and the gospel, but also raises questions about how we share the gospel and disciple new believers. Do we worship the same God? Was Mohammed demonic? Should we use the Qur'an in evangelism? To what extent does a convert have to disown Islam? When should a new believer be baptised? Is Islam capable of reformation? How do we understand the 'Insider Movement'? Being objective about these issues is very difficult indeed because they are so emotionally charged.

We need to appreciate and honour the contribution that those from a Muslim background can make, particularly in sharing with us the process by which they came to faith. What was important to them and the way that the Holy Spirit led them may well be the way he leads others; what was helpful and what a hindrance on their journey are valuable for us to hear.

However, and entirely understandably, believers from a Muslim background find it almost impossible to be objective about Islam. Emotionally, and in every other way, their lives have been intertwined with Islam. When they decided to follow Jesus, they probably experienced Islam at its worst. It may have caused them to lose their family, their inheritance, their job and their self-worth. They may have been physically attacked and verbally abused. They have probably been put under the most severe psychological pressure to return to Islam. No one who has been through these sorts of trauma can possibly be objective. Yet so often when churches want to learn about Islam, they assume that someone who was a Muslim would be the best person to tell them and provide an unbalanced view.

4 Encourage openness

In the past, Christians of different beliefs and persuasions have worked together by ignoring or not mentioning the things that they disagree about when they are together. This is not the policy of CRIB. In CRIB we do not cover over or ignore our differences; rather, we challenge the understanding of others, promote our own understanding and at the same time respect the opinions of others. Often we will get two people from different persuasions to speak, knowing that they disagree. We want to be able to understand their positions, but also demonstrate that they respect each other.

You will notice in the CRIB mission statement that the aim of building mutual respect is the second goal. This is because achieving the respect that is mentioned in goal number two is dependent on goal number one. It is difficult to have meaningful respect for people that you do not know. The whole process of building respect is dependent on some face-to-face time. We need to interact and to understand a person's background and culture. In establishing a network that is built on respect, it is necessary to arrange opportunities for sharing and interaction over a period of time.

5 Choose projects that include a wide spectrum of people

Our experience with CRIB suggests that a network that brings Christians together should have very focussed and very limited objectives. If you do undertake a project together, it must be one to which those of different persuasions can contribute.

In 2011, CRIB published a book entitled, "Between Naivety and Hostility – Uncovering the best Christian responses to Islam in Britain", and was edited by Steve Bell and Colin Chapman. (We wanted the subtitle to be 'Christian responses to Islam in Britain' – many felt that the subtitle our publisher chose was rather arrogant.) The book contained chapters written by 20 different people in the CRIB network. Colin Chapman was a very wise text editor. The project gave people a chance to present different positions, but again demonstrated the fact that we were committed to working together[2].

6 Make sure your network is accountable

Accountability within the Christian family is so important today. We should be wary of Christians in churches or in any other ministry who are not accountable. Some people say they are 'accountable to God', which of course we all are ultimately, but God has placed us in community so that we can be accountable to each other.

In the early days, CRIB joined the Evangelical Alliance in the UK. Later our accountability moved to Global Connections, but in both cases, we were giving these organisations the right to call us to account if anyone approached them with concerns about our beliefs or behaviour. The organisation that you choose to be accountable to is obviously important. It must not be too closely tied to a particular theology, churchmanship or Christian culture, because it needs the confidence of a broad range of Christian groups and churches.

Holding a network of strong-minded Christians together

If networks of Christians involved in Muslim ministry are going to develop across Europe, then the challenge will be how to disagree as Christian. What is absolutely certain is that there will be disagreements. We cannot get away from that nor can we ignore disagreements if we are committed to building networks in Christian fellowship.

The following suggestions for how we should disagree in a Christian way are based on a short paper of guidelines produced in the UK by a group committed to engaging in ministry to Muslims across the world, some of whom are involved in CRIB.

Basic assumptions within the Body of Christ

1. Don't assume that you will disagree with another Christian, but don't be surprised if you do.
2. If you do disagree, don't assume that the other person is wrong.
3. Because you disagree over one issue, don't assume that you will disagree over a lot of other things.
4. Put a charitable construction on issues where Christians think that there is doubt or vagueness, even if you believe it is perfectly clear.
5. Do not ridicule another person with whom you disagree. Do not malign people publically.

---

[2] Steve Bell and Colin Chapman (eds), *Between Naivety and Hostility – Uncovering the best Christian responses to Islam in Britain,* Authentic Copyright, 2011.

6. Try to de-personalise the issue. Help the disagreement to become a theoretical issue rather than a personal one (one Christian against another). To make this happen, you will probably need to involve others on both sides.
7. Respect those who strongly disagree with you, but for a variety of reasons do not wish to engage. Again, this is where the Body of Christ can help.

Common politeness and courtesy

There is certain behavior for which we need to strive.

1 Listen

Develop the skill of listening well. Listen carefully to what the other person has to say without interrupting. If you disagree, make sure you can express back to the person their argument in terms that they can agree with. If you can't do this face to face, express their argument in a document and ask them whether they agree with the contents.

Don't go by hearsay. Make sure you have read and understood what the other person has written on the subject.

2 Don't jump to assumptions about what people think

If someone says they believe something, it is easy to assume that they do not believe what you regard as the opposite view. That is the way our minds work, but it is not necessarily the way that Scripture works. Don't draw conclusions from what people do not say. Make sure what you are assuming a person believes, they would actually deny.

3 Make sure you are disagreeing about the right things

Many people disagree over small issues because they have very different views on bigger issues. There is little point in trying to come to agreement on a small area when there is an unidentified elephant in the room! Try to identify the key point of disagreement, rather than spending time on practical out-workings. Many people disagree about relating to or working with Muslims because they have a different understanding of the origins, nature and character of Islam.

4 Many of the issues that Christians disagree about are very complicated

There may be different ways of understanding a verse from Scripture or the balance of scriptural passages. There may be different cultural assumptions and understandings. In these complex issues, where many Christians feel that there could be a variety of right understandings, it is important to consider the motivation of the person with whom you disagree. Appreciate the right motivation even if you disagree with the conclusions.

5 If disagreement remains, so must respect

There will be times when we have to agree to differ. On these occasions, maintaining respect is very important (2 Thessalonians 3:15). The person we disagree with:

- Must not be attacked personally.
- Should be affirmed as a Christian.
- Should not have their ministry denigrated.
- Should not have their resources and sources of income sabotaged.

6 Careful about communication

If you write something about someone's ideas, let them see what you have written first. You may have the right to share your own opinions, but you do not have the right to circulate information that was not intended to be understood as fact. Be very careful about writing anything on an email or on a website. Things that you write can be forwarded on with additional comments to thousands of people who can easily pick up the wrong idea. Sadly, sometimes this has been done deliberately.

7 Pursue peace

We are followers of the Prince of Peace, we need to take seriously the strong emphasis of Scripture to live at peace, particularly with our brothers and sisters.

"Let us therefore make every effort to do what leads to peace and to mutual edification" (Romans 14:19). Verses that encourage peace include: Mark 9:50, Romans 12:18, 2 Corinthians 13:11, 1 Thessalonians 5:13, Hebrews 12:14, 1 Peter 3:11, 2 Timothy 2:22 and Colossians 3:15.

Summary

However much we may disagree with someone's beliefs, opinion, ministry or practice, as far as the individual is concerned there is no place for arrogance, impatience, a judgmental spirit, self-superiority, ridicule, contempt of others or a lack of compassion.

"When men have laboured as much in the improvement of the principle of forbearance as they have done to subdue other men to their opinions, religion will have another appearance in the World"[3]

---

[3] John Owen Vol. 13 p. 95, Banner of Truth, 1991.

Conclusion

Bert de Ruiter

There are many ways for Christians in Europe to engage with Muslims on our continent. Those discussed in this book are by no means the only ways to reach out to Muslims with the love of Christ. Other valid ministries exist, such as apologetics, ministry to Muslim children or social media and television to explain the Good News to Muslims.

In addition, there are many resources available, such as training materials, courses and books. We have made reference to specific books and articles, but many more have been published about Islam and about ways to reach out to Muslims with the Gospel.

We are thankful to God for those brothers and sisters who are engaged with Muslims in Europe – churches, Christians, missionaries from Europe and elsewhere – who are sharing their lives and the Gospel with Muslims. They need our prayers and our support.

It is encouraging that God brings Muslims to Christ in Europe and, although we didn't write about this in this book, we acknowledge the importance of discipling Muslim Background Believers to take up their role within existing churches and within new church plants across Europe. Some of the authors are involved in this ministry and are available to help churches in Europe with their expertise.

We have written this book with the aim to encourage all churches and Christians throughout Europe to become engaged with Muslims in Europe, according to their unique locations and giftings.

Most of the authors of this book work together as the European Ministry to Muslims Network of the European Leadership Forum. This network is a learning community of 10-15 Christians with a thorough knowledge of and ongoing practical involvement with Muslims in Europe. The members of the network represent a variety of approaches/methodologies regarding ministry to Muslims. Each member of the network has at least one specific expertise important in ministry to Muslims across Europe.

The members of the network seek to work in unity and to complement each other with their unique gifts and knowledge. We also work in collaboration with other local, national, regional and pan-European networks that focus on ministry to Muslims.

The network meet three times a year to: a) Identify the most pressing needs regarding ministry to Muslims in Europe and b) discuss how to help the church to address those needs; c) develop a deeper understanding of Muslims in Europe and to relate Biblical teaching to them with greater clarity and relevance.

Once a year, during the European Leadership Forum, we jointly provide training to those attending. Some of the training will be offered through webinars.

The members of the network regularly speak at conferences, training events, workshops, universities and theological seminaries etc. We offer our services to churches and Christians in Europe to equip them. We are also committed to mentor churches and Christians through onsite visits and webinars.

Our vision is to see a Church in Europe equipped to engage with Muslims with a compassionate heart, an informed mind, an involved hand and a witnessing tongue. We believe that through such engagement the Church not only will shape the future of Islam in Europe, but also will be used by Jesus Christ, the Head of the Church, to make many Muslims into His disciples. Whatever the form our engagement takes, we believes this to be its ultimate outcome.

List of Contributors

Dr. Bernhard Reitsma is professor of theology by Special Appointment at the VU University Amsterdam and senior lecturer at the Christian University of applied science in Ede, the Netherlands. He lived and worked in the Middle East, for almost eight years, lecturing in different theological universities and working with Lebanon Intervarsity. He publishes and teaches in the field of he Church in the context of Islam. Recently, his book *The God of my enemy. The Middle East and the Nature of God* (Regnum 2014) was published; a theological reflection on the challenges of the state of Israel for the Christian community in the Middle East.

Bernhard lives in the Netherlands; is married and has four children.

Dr. Bert de Ruiter is a staff worker of Operation Mobilization in Europe and the European Evangelical Alliance. He has been involved in Christian-Muslim relations in Europe for almost 30 years. He got an MA in World Evangelization and a D.Min. in Christian-Muslim relations. He has authored two books: "A Single Hand cannot applaud" on the value of the book of Proverbs in evangelizing Muslims and "Sharing Lives" on how Christians can overcome their fear of Islam and learn to share their lives with Muslims. He also has developed a course that is being used in several European countries, entitled Sharing Lives to help Christians share their lives with Muslims. Bert lives in Amsterdam, the Netherlands, is married and has two children and three grandchildren.

Dr. Efan Elias completed his PhD in 2008. Since then he has worked freelance. He is a regular consultant for government on identity issues and has written several papers for NGOs and think tanks. Efan's research has explored Western engagement with governance as well as examining questions of citizenship and identity for both Christians and Muslims.

Bryan Knell has been involved with Muslims and Islam for over 30 years. Firstly in the student world as a staff worker with UCCF with responsibilities for International Students. Following some theology, Bryan was then the UK Director of Arab World Ministries for 16 years and more recently he has been the coordinator of CRIB (Christian Responses to Islam in Britain). He has taught Christians about Islam at large festivals, in churches and in colleges. Bryan is married with 3 children and 7 grandchildren and when he has time he cycles and messes around in boats.

Dr. Elsie Maxwell has extensive experience in the world of Islam. She has been with Arab World Ministries since 1958 and has worked for 27 years in Algeria,

Tunisia, and Morocco. Since 1984 she has been working amongst Arabs in London while teaching Islamic courses at the London Bible College. Elsie meets and shares her faith with Arabic-speaking Muslim women and disciples young believers. A major part of her ministry is teaching, writing and training others for Muslim ministries.

Dr. Andreas Maurer is Islam Consultant with AVC (Action for persecuted Christians and needy people). After his training and work as a Mechanical Engineer in Switzerland, he studied at Bible College in England. Thereafter he enlarged his knowledge of Islam through various courses and theological studies at universities in England and South Africa. In 1999 he completed his doctorate at the University of Pretoria (UNISA) on the topic: «In Search of a new Life: Conversion Motives of Christians and Muslims». After working in South Africa from 15 years in projects concerning training Christians in mission to Muslims, he returned to Switzerland to work as an Islamicist with different organizations,. He has been training Christians in Muslim Evangelism worldwide. Andreas has written the book "Ask your Muslim friend". He is married to Ruth and has three sons

Anne-Käthi Degen wrote her MA about the Muslim youths scene in Switzerland. As a teacher and inter-religious youth worker she experienced secular Muslim teenagers as well as dedicated young Muslims. She initiated dialogue's work between Christian and Muslim youth groups. Now she's doing Post Graduate studies in "Interfaith Engagement" in England.

Ishak Ghatas is an Egyptian-born, studied theology in Belgium and currently is a PhD researcher at Oxford Centre for mission studies. Besides his pastoral work he has been involved in inter-religious dialogue at a variety of levels and with a variety of different actors. Ishak specializes in the different forms of Islam and Christianity, but is also well acquainted with the structures, philosophies and cultural specificities that underline the other major world religions. Currently he also is the religious expert to (ISPD) the International School of Protocol and Diplomacy of Brussels.

Hany Girgis is an Egyptian pastor. He is the founder of Arab Ministry in Spain, an initiative to reach out and interact with the Arab immigrant community. Through twenty years of work of service, the ministry grew to two social centers, and planted the first Arabic speaking church in Spain. Hany is a PhD candidate. He is conducting a research on "Immigration and Faith Interaction", which focuses on developing the dialogue and interactions between Evangelicals and Muslims in Europe, especially in Spain.

Paul Sydnor is EU Director of the International Association for Refugees. He has been serving refugees since 1985. He served with Operation Mobilisation (1 year), Slavic Gospel Association (3 years) and International Teams (15

years). He began serving with IAFR in 2010. He is an active founding member of the Refugee Highway Partnership in Europe. Having served as a pastor, Paul's focus has been to help local churches to reach out to refugees in meaningful ways. He has helped empower and activate church-based work among refugees in several places around Europe including, Austria, Italy, France, Germany and the UK. He has come alongside of a number of refugee leaders over the years to strengthen and support them in their own efforts, including refugee leaders from Croatia, Kosovo, Iran, Iraq, Afghanistan, Syria and several parts of Africa. Paul is working on a Ph.D. at the Oxford Centre for Mission Studies (OCMS). Paul and his family live in northern France. His wife is from Germany. They have raised their three teenage kids in 3 European countries.

Bert de Ruiter

A Single Hand Cannot Applaud
The Value of Using the Book of Proverbs in Sharing the Gospel with Muslims

Christians who want to share the truth about God with their Muslim friends understandably try to encourage them to read the Bible. Unfortunately, many Muslims believe that Jews and Christians have corrupted the books that God has given them. As a consequence, Muslims are hesitant about reading the Bible. Given this antagonism among a large percentage of Muslims towards Christianity in general and the Bible in particular, there is a need to prepare the ground before a Muslim can be persuaded to read the Bible.

To stimulate Muslims to read the Scriptures, we need to find common ground between their world view and the Bible. This book argues that we find such common ground in the book of Proverbs. The universal character of the book of Proverbs makes it a useful bridge between the truth of God and those outside the Christian faith, including Muslims. The use of proverbs is very common in many Muslim cultures. God's wisdom found in the book of Proverbs resembles the content of proverbial sayings in many Muslim cultures. Therefore using this book as a tool in sharing theWord of God with Muslims can create openings where there were none. Muslims are familiar with the Solomon of Scripture because he is mentioned in the Qur'an, but most have never read his words. The wisdom God gave Solomon is a natural link to Muslim people so they can come to know more about God. The book of Proverbs is one of the most valuable tools, particularly in combination with local proverbs, to lead our Muslim friends from accepting familiar truth, to embrace less familiar truth, and then to worship the One who said "I am the truth" (John 14:6).

Pb. • pp. 90 • £ 8.00 • $ 12.99 • € 9.50
ISBN 978-3-941750-07-4

VTR Publications • Gogolstr. 33 • 90475 Nürnberg • Germany
info@vtr-online.com • http://www.vtr-online.com

Bert de Ruiter

Sharing Lives

Overcoming Our Fear of Islam

This book argues that the single greatest hindrance to Christian witness amongst Muslims in Europe is fear.

Many European Christians fear that Europe will gradually turn into Eurabia, or Islamic domination of Europe, and they ignore the efforts of Muslims to adapt to the European context, a situation pointing to a future scenario of Euro-Islam, or Islam being Europeanized. The author argues that instead of an attitude of fear, which leads to exclusion, Christians should develop an attitude of grace, which leads to embrace.

After analyzing books and courses developed to help Christians relate to Muslims, he concludes that these mostly concentrate on providing information and skills, instead of dealing with one's attitude. Because of this the author developed a short course to help Christians overcome their fear of Islam and Muslims and to encourage Christians to share their lives with Muslims and to share the truth of the Gospel.

Pb. • pp. XIII + 209 • £ 13.95 • $ 22.95 • € 14.90
ISBN 978-3-941750-22-7

VTR Publications • Gogolstr. 33 • 90475 Nürnberg • Germany
info@vtr-online.com • http://www.vtr-online.com

Deborah Meroff

Europe: Restoring Hope

The continent known for over 1000 years as the heartland of Christianity has gone into spiritual arrest. Drawing from the experience of many individuals and organisations, this book takes a hard look at four population groups at the centre of Europe's heart trouble: marginalised people, Muslims, youth and nominal and secular Europeans. Here is proof that it is possible to restore hope to this great continent when God's people work together. This practical resource supplies all the motivation and information we need to get started.

"Europe is very likely a battleground for the future of global Christianity... I hope that whoever reads these pages will be encouraged and inspired to prayer and action."

Jirí Unger, President of the European Evangelical Alliance

"My wife Drena and I have now been based in Europe for 50 years. Debbie Meroff's book True Grit was one of the most important books in our lives, and her new book on Europe is another cutting edge, must-read!"

George Verwer, Founder and International Co-ordinator Emeritus, OM International

"This book shows that God is still at work in Europe. He is building his church despite many challenges. And he wants to see each one of us playing an active part in restoring hope to Europe!"

Frank Hinkelmann, European Director, OM International

Pb. • pp. VIII + 295 • £ 14.95 • $ 24.95 • € 14.95
ISBN 978-3-941750-06-7

VTR Publications • Gogolstr. 33 • 90475 Nürnberg • Germany
info@vtr-online.com • http://www.vtr-online.com

www.ingramcontent.com/pod-product-compliance
Lightning Source LLC
Chambersburg PA
CBHW071713040426
42446CB00011B/2042